Norman Potter

What is a designer

: things . places . messages

Hyphen Press . London

First published by Studio Vista, London, and Van Nostrand Reinhold
    Company, New York, in 1969
Revised and extended second edition published by Hyphen Press, Reading,
    in 1980
Revised third edition published by Hyphen Press, London, in 1989
This fourth edition published by Hyphen Press, London, in 2002; reprinted
    with minor corrections in 2003, 2006

The book was designed by Françoise Berserik, The Hague. The text was
typeset and made into pages by Teus de Jong, Nij Beets, in Adobe InDesign.
The text was output in the typeface Arnhem, designed by Fred Smeijers,
Antwerp. The book was made and printed in the Netherlands by Koninklijke
Wöhrmann BV, Zutphen

ISBN 0–907259–16–2
ISBN 978–0–907259–16–9

www.hyphenpress.co.uk

To Mark, †1969, and those with him at Bristol, Hornsey, Guildford

Sequence of parts

Architecture is organization. *You are an organizer, not a drawing-board stylist.*
    Le Corbusier

Woe to the man whose heart has not learned while young to hope, to love – and to put its trust in life.
    Joseph Conrad

The disciplinary barriers are impenetrable. If these barriers in education were to vanish, the architect as benevolent dictator would vanish too. Instead students could arm themselves with useful tools and knowledge with which they could assist a community.
    Tom Woolley

Sources for these and other references are given in part 23

Introduction

This is a book for students who design artefacts of the kind studied in design and architectural schools. Aside from the question implicit in its title, it asks what skills and aptitudes may be appropriate to the practice of design. A general discussion of such matters, including detailed recommendations for further reading, is followed by a directly practical reference section, confined to essentials, on various aspects of design technique (distinguished by a change of page colour). The absence of pictures is deliberate and considered. The reasons will become apparent to any thoughtful reader, as the argument of the book develops, but there is a terse summary of this reasoning in part 19 ('Questioning design'; see pages 158–9 particularly).

By the word 'student' I mean to include those of all ages coming freshly to their subject. At a certain level of awareness all creative workers gain in humility as their knowledge develops, and will wish frequently to return to their origins for refreshment of the spirit: to ask yet again who they are, what they could or should be doing, and why. I would like to think that this book will be a congenial companion to any engaged by such a quest, as much as to those who, starting their journey, turn to it for guidance.

It is well enough understood that design is a socially negotiated discipline, and there are telling respects in which design questions are political questions. No book about design is politically value-free, whatever its apparent claim to objectivity. I would like to make it plain, therefore, that this book has always belonged resolutely with the standpoint of the libertarian left, and still does so. It is a textbook of design, not a political tract; but that is its standpoint. It also adopts and explores – even more unfashionably – a generally modernist position in that context, holding that 'like the poor (it seems), what is modern is always with us; and open to transformation'. Constructive forces in the world should not be confused with those of reaction, but there is nothing very new in such conflicts; nor in the difficulty of their interpretation.

7

There are certain very general facts of modern life, within which any constructive activity must he seen as contributory. Untouched by them, any such activity is perhaps better suited to garden gnomes than to human beings. These facts include a global view of the human situation, which can hardly exclude the decimation of the rain forests any more than the appalling disparity of living standards, and life expectation, in the different parts of our world; not to speak of the nerve-centres in the self-awareness of our time, which have been the revelations of the concentration camps and the terrible lurking ever-present destructive threat of the Bomb – now so inconceivably destructive even in one warhead as to defy imagining. Yet if human solidarity and humane imagining mean anything at all, it is upon such awareness that every act of construction, however small, must in some sense draw, seek nourishment, become predicated – or withdraw into triviality and the blandishments of excess. A certain order of sensibility, if not of commitment, belongs to such perceptions; and a different one, to their suppression, or neutering. To expose and to clarify, not to embellish, was at once the joy and the seriousness of the modern movement, and it remains vital to its task and heritage.

To some of these questions, and to the underlying problems of industrialism as such, E. F. Schumacher has brought a notable diagnostic acumen as much as simplicity of heart, putting in very simple language what must surely be plain:

'There are four main characteristics of modern industrial society which, in the light of the Gospels, must be accounted four great and grievous evils:

1   Its vastly complicated nature.
2   Its continuous stimulation of, and reliance on, the deadly sins of greed, envy, and avarice.
3   Its destruction of the content and dignity of most forms of work.
4   Its authoritarian character, owing to organization in excessively large units.

All these evils are, I think, exacerbated by the fact that the bulk of industry is carried on for the purpose of private pecuniary gain ... [but] the worst exploitation practised today is "cultural exploitation", namely, the exploitation by unscrupulous moneymakers of the deep longing for culture on the part of the less privileged and undereducated groups in our society.'

Schumacher also had constructive offerings, not necessarily to the taste or within the aptitude of many designers, but since in this book I am arguing that 'design is a field of concern, response, and enquiry as often as decision and consequence' – big words! – it may be encouraging to remember that we still have visible role-models within a radical Christian attitude. Trendies take note.

It remains to ask, in an introductory spirit, what is special about this book, and justifies a new edition. First, it is original: that is to say written at first hand from my own experience as a designer, maker, and teacher; rather than from reading other books. It is useful, I think – useful evidentially to students – to have felt the modern movement in your bones, to have lived it. Such 'being original' is not exclusively useful, however. Creative critical scholarship – to which I have little claim – has something different to offer, and complementary: the special benefit of breadth, distance, and relative impartiality of view. This brings me to a second foundation asset of this book. Like – I suggest – the root impulse and need of truly modern design, it is not self-contained; it is contributory. There are other books by scholars, and many books of pictures. The first thing to learn about the deep structure of modern design is that it is *relation-seeking* and pleasurably so; but that, as the saying is, we shall come to. Good work was probably always difficult, and recently never more so; but I hope this book will encourage those who hold to it.

1   What *is* a designer?

Design:
v. to mark out; to plan, purpose, intend ...
n. a plan conceived in the mind, of something to be done ...
n. adaptation of means to end ...
   The shorter Oxford English dictionary

Every human being is a designer. Many also earn their living by design – in every field that warrants pause, and careful consideration, between the conceiving of an action and a fashioning of the means to carry it out, and an estimation of its effects.

In fact this book is concerned mainly – not wholly – with a minority profession: of designers whose work helps to give form and order to the amenities of life, whether in the context of manufacture, or of place and occasion. The very clumsiness of this definition underlines the difficulty of using one word to denote a wide range of quite disparate experiences – both in the outcome of design decisions, and in the activity of designing. The dictionary reference above is selective; in practice the word is also applied to the *product* of 'a plan conceived in the mind', not only as a set of drawings or instructions, but as the ultimate outcome from manufacture.

This is confusing. The difficulty becomes acute if the word 'design' is used without reference to any specific context – used, for instance, as a blanket term to cover every situation in which adaptation of means to ends is preceded by an abstract of intent – though designing is thus usefully distinguished from 'making' or from spontaneous activity. Beyond this point, the word must refer to recognizable products and opportunities, or become hopelessly abstract.

The design work to be discussed is now usually studied within the art and design faculty of a polytechnic, in a school of architecture, sometimes within a university, and – not least – in some of the smaller art and design colleges that may provide vocational courses. 'Distance-learning' institutions may provide study courses, necessarily at a generalized level and without the benefit of studios and workshops. And of course, with or without the aid of such studies and evening classes, it is perfectly possible to study design simply by doing it. It should not be necessary to say that architects are designers (even if the matter is, occasionally, in doubt). Taking that old stand-by the 'broad view', it is convenient to group the work into three simple categories, though the distinctions are in no way absolute, nor are they always so described: product design (things), environmental design (places) and communication design (messages). Such categories blur some further necessary distinctions (as between, for instance, the design of industrial equipment and that of retail products in a domestic market) but can form a useful departure.

In the field of product design, the professional extremes might be said to range from studio pottery and textile design at one end of the spectrum to engineering design and computer programming at the other. This is a very broad spectrum and clearly there are serious differences at the extremes. In the communication field, a similar spectrum might range from, say, freehand book illustration, to the very exact disciplines of cartography or the design of instrumentation for aircraft.

Obviously, the more aesthetic and sensory latitude available within a particular range of design opportunities, the closer they resemble those offered by the practice of 'fine-art'. The less latitude, the closer design becomes to the sciences, and to fields in which the scope of aesthetic 'choice' is truly marginal. The design of a traffic light system has an aesthetic component, but it would need a very special definition of aesthetics to embrace the many determining factors that must finally settle the design outcome.

The situation for architects is usually held to be more straightforward; historically, their position has developed a fairly clear set of responsibilities. However, the complex changes in building types, and in industrialized building possibilities, have combined with other factors thoroughly to upset this stable picture. Indeed, the architect's work has been so undermined by that of specialists in surrounding territory (engineers, planners, sociologists, interior designers, etc.) that the profession is no longer so easy to identify. It is still reasonable to see an architect as a designer with a specialized technical and functional competence, and again a spectrum is discernible, ranging from very open and ephemeral design situations, to those as critical as the design of an operating theatre.

It is necessary to start somewhere, and this book takes a middle-zone standpoint. In most art schools this will include furniture, interior design, exhibition design, packaging, some wide areas of graphic and industrial (product) design, and some of the fringe territory leading into architecture. Students must make the necessary allowances to accommodate their own subject of study. This is chiefly necessary in part 2 ('Is a designer an artist?') and in some of the notes on procedure (parts 11–16) – or the studio potter will certainly feel that everything in this book is unduly complicated, whereas an architect might feel that there is undue simplification. All designers, however specialized should know roughly what their colleagues do – and why; not only to fertilize their own thinking, but also to make group practice effective, and for other reasons that will appear.

There are many roles for designers even within a given sector of professional work. A functional classification might be: impresarios, culture diffusers, culture generators, assistants, and parasites. Impresarios: those who get work, organize others to do it, and present the outcome. Culture diffusers: those who do competent work effectively over a broad field, usually from a stable background of dispersed interests. Culture generators: obsessive characters who work in back rooms and produce ideas, often more useful to other designers than the public. Assistants: often beginners, but also a large group concerned with administration or draughtsmanship. Parasites: those who skim off the surface of other people's work and make a good living by it. The first four groups are interdependent, necessary to each other. It should be added that any designer might shift from one role to another in the course of his working life, or even within the development of a single commission, though temperament and ability encourage a more permanent separation of functions in a large design office. Thus no value-judgement is implied here, except upon parasites who are only too numerous.

In small offices – or of course for independent freelance workers – there will be little stratification; 'the office' may tend to move in one direction or another, but the work within it will be less predictable for any one member – excluding, perhaps, secretarial or administrative assistants and often temporary draughtsmen. A 'consultant' is often a lone wolf who deals in matters of high expertise or (paradoxically) of very broad generality. Designers will be found in every quarter, sometimes working independently, sometimes for government or local authority offices, or attached to large manufacturers, to retail agencies, to public corporations, and elsewhere in places too numerous to mention. Artisan designers will have their own workshop and perhaps their own retail outlet. There are a few design offices that will design anything from a fountain pen to an airport, and will therefore employ specialists from every field (including architects) – a rational development and a welcome one, but implying some genius for large scale organization which, in turn, may tend to level out the standard of work produced. (As numbers increase, it becomes a problem to keep work flowing through at a productive pace, yet have enough – not too much – to allow everyone a fair living.) Students usually need a few years' office practice before setting up by themselves; often this happens in small groups of three to six designers who will share office and administrative expenses.

Most designers are educated in a formal way by three-to-seven years in a design school (or school of architecture) leading to appropriate qualifications. Some have had unorthodox beginnings – by dropping in the deep end and learning to swim – but self-training may need sympathetic patrons, is apt to be patchy according to the opportunities that occur, and needs a special pertinacity. Apprenticeship rarely means more than training as a draughtsman. A few factories or retail firms may encourage employees who show design aptitude. Evening classes and correspondence courses are mostly directed at cultural appreciation or do-it-yourself horizons, but intending full-time students can build up a portfolio of work by this means.

A note of warning: the word 'design' appears freely as noun and verb, and where words like 'formal', 'realization', 'consciousness' are used without qualification, readers should examine the context and think for themselves. I have used the word 'student' suggestively; trying it for size.

There is a perfectly good sense in which a creative worker remains, perpetually a humble student of his subject. This is not to be confused with the timidity of the 'permanent student' whose name haunts the lists of application for grants, research funds, and finally, minor teaching appointments. These must again be distinguished from the serious student of scholarly bent who 'reads' the subject and may make a distinctive contribution to theory or criticism. By the word 'student', therefore, I mean those who still question what they are doing, and ask why.

There is no word by the use of which sex-discrimination can be avoided. Readers must accept that when 'him' or 'man' is used, these words embrace both sexes (unless the text does draw a distinction). Women should not be deterred from course-work that includes the use of machinery and unfamiliar work with hand-tools. Invariably such skills are gained rapidly and practised with enthusiasm.

This, then, is the apparent situation of the designer and where this book begins. Returning to the statement that every human is a designer, and using it as a springboard: we do well to remember that designers are ordinary human beings, as prone as others (given half a chance) to every human weakness, including an exaggerated idea of their own consequence. Consider the following questions: Should a designer design for a factory in which he could never imagine working as an operative? Is design social-realist art? Is it handy to be in a state of moral grace when designing a knife and fork? Does design work justify its claims to social usefulness, or is it a privileged form of self-expression? Is a profession a genteel self-protection society with some necessary illusions? Should a designer be a conformist or an agent of change?

Those who feel that such questions are diversionary and a waste of time, should perhaps put this book down; others read on, but not for easy answers.

2   Is a designer an artist?

Before discussing this question, which involves describing a designer's work in some detail, it is necessary to look at the context in which it is usually asked. First, each country or culture has its own history, and this must affect how design functions now in any particular culture. The second difficulty is more widespread. It is the well-known but uneasy juxtaposition of 'fine-art' studies with 'design' subjects within a common faculty, excluding (normally) architecture. It would be out of place here to examine the history of this problematic and to some extent (now) arbitrary grouping of studies. It is enough to point out that the situation could be more realistically appraised if painting and sculpture were studied alongside music, dance, poetry, film and other activities that interpret, primarily, the psychological and sensuous and spiritual understanding of man. It would then be easier to distinguish those activities which must first satisfy his physical and accessory needs under conditions of complex social constraint (as in building design), or which may have a much humbler role in serving and pleasing man. It is true that, in the last analysis, every human artefact – whether painting, poem, chair, or rubbish bin – evokes and invokes the inescapable totality of a culture, and the hidden assumptions which condition cultural priorities. (In a basic sense, and given the conditions for warmth, food and shelter, the rest is a choice and speaks to us of priorities which need constant revaluation.) For the purpose of the remarks which follow, it is certainly necessary to say that if the words 'fine-art' and 'design' simply refer to a duality as experienced in art schools, it is difficult to set up satisfactory distinctions on that basis alone.

For the discussion that follows, the situation is seen from the standpoint of a designer.

Here is a sober but accurate description of professionalism by Misha Black: '... the offering to the public of a specialized skill, depending largely upon judgement, in which both the experience and established knowledge are of equal weight, while the person possessing the skill is bound both by an ethical code and may be accountable at law for a proper degree of skill in exercising this judgement.'

Not, obviously, a full description, and perhaps a somewhat negative one, but making the fact plain that a designer works through and for other people, and is concerned primarily with their problems rather than his own. In this respect he might be seen as a medical man, with the responsibility a doctor has for accurate diagnosis (problem analysis) and for a relevant prescription (design proposals), though the comparison should not be taken too far. It must be clearly realized that designers work and communicate indirectly, and their creative work finally takes the form of instructions to contractors, manufacturers and other executants. The exception is the designer-craftsman or artisan, whose situation is discussed in part 6. The instructions may include written specifications, reports, and other documents, detailed working drawings, presentation drawings for clients, scale models and sometimes prototypes in full size. Since this is as far as a designer goes in direct production (strictly what he makes are visual analogues), it is necessary that the instructions are very clear, complete, and in other ways acceptable to those who must work from them. Much is said about this requirement in parts 11 to 16 of this book.

The designer usually has the further responsibility of supervising the work, but there is no obvious equivalent for the feedback through eye-and-hand so familiar to the painter or sculptor, whereby the original idea is constantly developed, enriched, or diverted by the actual experience of the materials and the making-process. The artisan is an exception. For most designers the point of no return (commitment to final drawings) is indeed final, unless everything is upset by site contingencies. So-called 'feedback' does of course operate at the design stage, mainly through people, circumstance, and the continuous absorption of new information into the design brief, which will alter its definition. The outcome will still change radically from first ideas thrown up by superficial acquaintance with the design problem, but the changes will not always be of the designer's own choosing: their nature may be objectively determined by factors quite outside his control. Such factors might be something to do with costs, the availability of materials or techniques, a change in the client's requirements, or simply the discovery of factors that were hidden from sight in the early stages of the job.

Hence, in summary, the designer provides instructions (having exhaustively established and agreed the best course of action), and the work necessarily involves many different people whose interests (often in conflict) he must seek to reconcile. With some such people he may have (legally) contractual relationships.

Thus many specific responsibilities may arise – to clients, contractors, to the public who use the end-product, to numerous specialists or colleagues who may be involved if the undertaking is a large one (which implies team-work and frequently shared decisions). If it is a building, it mustn't fall down; if it is a chair, it mustn't be thirty inches high, have an innate tendency to collapse under load, it mustn't employ joints that can't be made except by special machinery (unless this can be found economical) and it mustn't cost so much as to be unmarketable. The designer cannot exercise personal insights until every apparently conflicting factor in his brief has been reconciled to best advantage: until, in short, he knows exactly what he is up against and which constraints can be made to play in his favour.

For such reasons, the designer is highly 'problem' conscious; a large part of his work may consist in problem analysis, though rarely of the complex order familiar in the sciences. To an ability for sorting, ordering, and relating information he must bring qualities of judgement and discrimination as much as a lively imagination. There is a diffuse sense in which the most seemingly 'objective' procedures in problem analysis are in practice discretionary, embedded as they are in the whole matrix of professional judgement in which relevant decisions are conceived. In some fields (such as textile design) there is far greater latitude than in others. In most design work the ultimate decisions affect, in a vital degree, appearance; but the look of the job, however lovingly considered, will emerge from, and in some sense express, the functional and circumstantial background. There are of course cases in which a communication requirement will be superimposed overridingly upon other factors, like structural logic; that would simply be a special (perhaps sophisticated) view of function.

Drawings can never be an end for a designer (excepting an

illustrator); they are a means to the end of manufacture, and their expressive content is strictly limited to the purposes of relevant communication. This obvious distinction from fine-art drawing can easily be overlooked in a design school where the design projects are theoretical, and drawings become the only outcome, acquiring the false dignity of an end-product in the process. This does not imply that drawings can be loveless, slovenly, or inadequate in any way, but that their nature is strictly purposeful. It may indeed be necessary to the designer to make loving, scrupulous and over-adequate drawings for his own self-satisfaction and to preserve his own standards. Only in this sense are design drawings 'self-expression'.

At every stage of design there will be discussion, questions and argument; the final design will have to be demonstrated and if necessary defended to the client, who will not understand what the final result will look like, but will naturally tend to assume that he knows more about his own problems than does the designer – despite having called him in to solve them. A design proposal intermingles with the world of considerations familiar to the client; communication media must be carefully chosen – verbal reports and other documents may accompany drawings and models. Designers use words constantly and in direct relation to their work; in forming and discussing ideas, assessing situations, annotating drawings, writing specifications and letters, and in report writing. This aspect of design work is frequently underestimated: an ability to use words clearly, pointedly, and persuasively is at all times relevant to design work.

It is now possible to ask, what kind of person might be happy and personally fulfilled in taking up design? It will be seen that a designer must be capable of more detachment than may be necessary to a fine-artist. He must be able to weigh up a problem, or an opportunity, in a dispassionate way, on its terms (as well as his own), and to select, arrange, and dispose his decisions accordingly. He must be able to thrive on constraint and to turn every opportunity to good account. He must like and understand people and be able to treat with them; he must be able to accept fairly complex situations in which he may well be working as a member of a team. He must be reasonably articulate. He must be practical and prepared for extensive responsibilities to other people. Finally he must be prepared to spend at least half his time working with graphic media, since most design work appears in drawings of one sort or another when decisions have been finalized.

These remarks may suggest an uncomfortably glum idea of human perfectibility. In practice, of course a designer's life is as muddled, informal, and accident-prone, as most people's lives manage to be; not only behind the scenes, but sometimes in front of them. Every profession has roughly defined public responsibilities, which are met as closely as possible by accepted codes of practice. Again, the fact that design work is ten per cent inspiration and ninety per cent fairly hard work – not an unusual prospect – does need some well-organized procedures to keep the brief clearly in view, and the available energies best occupied.

Some of these procedures will be familiar to painters and sculptors, and certainly to film-makers; but for them the work will have a more inward character in its origins. Thus a painter's first responsibility is to the truth of his own vision, even though that vision may (or maybe always does) change as his work proceeds. He may be involved with contractual responsibilities, but not to the same extent as is a designer, whose decisions will be crucially affected by them. The designer works with and for other people: ultimately this may be true of the fine-artist, but in the actual working procedure a designer's formative decisions have a different order of freedom. The fine-artist is less dependent on discussion, agreement, letters, visits: the apparatus of communication that brings definition to a design problem, and relevance to its solution. A fine-artist usually works directly with his materials, or with a very close visual analogue to the final work. As we have seen, the designer has a long way to go before firm proposals can emerge – and even then a model may be the nearest thing to a tangible embodiment of his ideas.

In the case of film, television, and theatre, which might be described as a realm of public art, quite complex design procedures are involved. In the main, however, the real connection between fine-artists and designers springs from the benefit of a shared visual sensibility; not from a relevant or direct transference of skills, language, or formative insight, from one field to the other. Students are warned that this is an opinion: recalling the breadth of the design 'spectrum', they will see that this is a difficult matter to unravel. So

19

many factors impinge on the visual appearance of a design outcome that a designer's hand would seem to be guided by a wholly different 'requiredness' (a term borrowed from Gestalt psychology) from that which informs a painting or a work of sculpture. Yet there are component experiences with something in common. Equally valid transferences may occur from the 'feel' of related work in other fields (for example, philosophy, music, or mathematics) and should be encouraged to do so. Similarly, a creative sensibility may derive from unlikely sources that cannot be looked for in any one field alone.

It is only necessary to hammer home the obvious because fine-art and design (excepting architecture) are often taught as closely interrelated subjects, and students are asked to choose between them. The isolation of architecture, which has always been the home base of design theory, is hard to explain and justify. Perhaps the theory is affected by it. The term 'fine-art' is unpleasantly genteel, but will be met with in the careers prospectuses and in the art schools, normally to comprise painting, sculpture, printmaking, and photography, and to distinguish these studies from 'applied art', in the various fields of design discussed here. The view that there is a parallel situation in the sciences, as between pure science and applied technology, is a questionable one: equally untrustworthy is the supposition that painting, sculpture, industrial design, architecture, derive in some sense from the common fountain-head of 'art'. To suggest this seriously requires a view of art (and a set of definitions) quite outside the scope of the present discussion: it is partly a semantic problem, pointing to the inadequacy of ordinary descriptive language. Without distorting common usage, it might be said that designers are content to bring a certain artistry to their work, and to recognize that there is much in common between the few masters in any field – fine-art, design, science, medicine, philosophy – more, perhaps, than unites the very disparate standards that coexist in any one profession.

3   Design education: principles

'Well building hath three conditions: commoditie, firmnes,
and delight'
    Vitruvius / Sir Henry Wotton

'Love, work and knowledge are the wellsprings of our life.
They should also govern it'
    Wilhelm Reich

A design capability proceeds from a fusion of skills, knowledge,
understanding, and imagination; consolidated by experience. These
are heavy words, and they refer to the foundations. We accept a certain minimal competence as the basis of professional self-respect,
and as some guarantee of a designer's usefulness to other people.
Within limits such a competence is definable, and will begin to
form outlines within a formally structured teaching/learning situation. It is too much to say outright that design ability can be 'taught'.
As with any other creative activity, it is a way of doing things that can
only be grown into, perhaps – but not necessarily – in the context of
a formal design education.

    This view is readily conceded for something as immaterial as
'imagination', but it is commonly held that skills and knowledge
must not only be taught, but rigorously examined: if only to protect
an unsuspecting society against social or technical malpractice.
Defensible as this may be, it is not an assumption that should
go unquestioned, nor deflect attention from the weaknesses of received professional standards. The damage caused by knowledge
used without understanding is merely difficult to measure: it is not
less real for that. A skill may be irrelevant to the nature of a problem,
or – in dealing with people – may be grossly uninstructed in a necessary tact and discernment. Knowledge may be thinly experienced as
a rag-bag of conventional responses helped along by access to someone else's published working details. Plainly, skill and knowledge
cannot be weighed out by the pound, and separated from qualitative

perceptions, for any but the simplest mechanical problems – and even there it is questionable. Even 'judgement', that wise old word, becomes ponderously inhuman unless fertilized by some order of creative spontaneity.

Architecture is only one profession that offers uncomfortable testimony in these respects. It is nice to know, for instance, that a building is unlikely to leak or fall down (in fact someone else has probably done the calculations) and in a simple way this must be counted a social gain. On the other hand there are very many thousands of architects all of whom have passed their examinations, and can we decently say that more than a substantial minority produce buildings of affective quality? Of course their work is sometimes exceedingly difficult and subject to every conceivable restriction, but does their education help them to feel desperately a gap between promise and fulfilment, and thus to find every conceivable way of bridging it?

Let us answer (to be charitable) that the best schools know this problem backwards and do their best to resolve it. A 'profession' can still become a self-protection society with a very short term view of the priorities for professional competence. In the long term, we have no yardstick for the spirit of man and the nature of deprivations in his environment – not only the wilderness he may see and accept all around him, but the very nature of his interaction with a wholeness of experience, of which a built environment is but a part.

These are large thoughts, and will surely bring a smile to the face of any over-worked architectural assistant, aware as he is of the drudge component that occupies so much of his conscientious labours. Yet to evaluate formal design education it is necessary to ask some awkward questions. Not only to disturb our unthinking acceptance of social norms, but to bring some very practical matters sharply into focus, and others to dismiss as marginally relevant. For instance, our assistant would confirm that much of his work is elaborately interwoven with building contingencies and the structure of 'consents' which sometimes keeps him awake at night; the personality of the local district surveyor may occasionally seem the most omnipresent factor in the whole of the job. It is impossible to explain this properly to a student in a school; you simply need the experience of design practice to see how it happens, and just what you do to keep the job moving and your first intentions reasonably intact, or, as is often the case, subtly changing as new possibilities reveal themselves. The way in which accidents of site contingency suddenly appear as benefits, so the designer wonders why he hadn't thought of that in the first place – to explain *that* as part of the 'design process' is really not at all easy.

It is also desirable (to put it mildly) to see the educational problem in terms of the future as much as the present – and, in rather a different way, in terms of the past. It would be a mistake to presuppose a static social situation, pleasantly unified in the untroubled pursuit of affluence, disturbed at most by some new concession to the good life announced in the weekly journals, and the designer providing his expensive austerities where they can be afforded; namely, in the places of high financial decision-making. Such banalities may go sour before the last Barcelona chair is glued into position to impress – who? There were signs in 1968, if not now, that young people were certainly less impressed than some of their parents. Yet a measurable standard of living is not to be despised because not all of us have it or want it, when millions of people desire above all some alleviation of their physical poverty. Nor can we play God and start back from square one with a wholesale redistribution of resources and an imposed system of moral absolutes to keep everything tidy. In short, the designer, like other honest citizens, will need access to faith and vision as much as to a keen analytical intelligence – to engage with life effectively, and to make something good through work. Aside from a technical training, what can a design school do to help?

This is not easy; a simplistic approach helps nobody. Hence the paragraphs that follow.

A first requirement for students is knowledge of how they can best help *themselves*: in this respect it is useful to understand the limits and benefits of an academic situation. To begin with, students should realize that both education and design practice are too often handicapped by identity-fixations. The words by which people describe themselves – architect, graphic designer, interior designer, etc. – become curiously more important than the work they actually do. In one respect this is fair, because under modern conditions it may be very difficult to find one word to identify their work, but such words tend to build up irrelevant overtones of meaning which are more useful as a comfort to personal security than as a basis for co-operative enterprise. Such confusions interpenetrate with status values and the other intricate strands of our social life, so it is hardly surprising that education is affected by them. Thus it comes about that design education is often still irrationally divided up into specializations with a doubtful relation to the work students may finally do, and with even less plausible reference to the situation *as it could be* in ten years' time.

This is not in itself the case for a generalist education – the silliness of outdated categories is a negative consideration – nor can matters be improved by denying that specific subjects relevantly exist, and that they are worth studying in depth. In theory, of course, a three-year study programme could investigate the Universe from the confines of a single problem. It is also a fallacy of bad technical training – as implied earlier – to suppose that skills and knowledge can be picked up 'in vacuo' or in neat packages as in a supermarket; such knowledge is sometimes used with a contempt and a restlessness that betrays the additive nature of its learning. Thus a restless and dissatisfied student who seeks his freedom in the extent, rather than the depth, of his explorations, may be dancing to the tune of the masters he is trying to escape from (whether such masters are real or imaginary). Skills ought to keep pace with understanding, and thus emerge organically; and the spread of lateral thinking must be complemented by vertical thinking (and dreaming) of a quite different kind, if understanding is to grow from strong roots. It is also a mistake to think that good design (or creative thinking of any kind) has much to do with a perfectly fitted-out environment. Much design work can be approached with freshness and insight with very little in the way of equipment and materials: the assumption to the contrary (as an accepted starting point for design) merely reflects a social climate in which the least meaning emerges for a gross expenditure of effort and apparatus.

It is a sad but interesting observation that the most rigidly blinkered courses of 'training' are often the least technically competent, rather in the way that some committed amateurs do better work than tradesmen who have lost a responsible relation to their trades. ('Amateur' – one who loves.) Even if it were not so, an education should always be why-responsive (and thus, question itself), whereas of its nature, a training asks how, and provides tidy answers. In either case, however, the best theoretical framework for studies will be alive or dead rigid, according to the spirit in which it is interpreted, both by students and staff, which in turn is a function of confidence within the academic community.

Although this discussion is tending to assume that the schools and colleges are where it all happens, Ivan Illich reminds us that it is easy to confuse schooling with education, when in fact education is a natural life-process and some schools may actually be anti-educative. A certain realism of outlook is required, if the schools are to be seen for what they are. A design school may be in some sense preparatory for life to follow, but a student's time there is precious and irrecoverable life in the present. It is also, however, a safe berth in harbour. In a somewhat different way, the staff of a school seek their own expression in the achievement of the school; it is their own chosen and continuing way of life. On the whole, the work is agreeable, relatively well paid, and socially well regarded. It is work that allows some teachers to defer indefinitely a close look at their own inadequacies. For many reasons – not all so uncharitable – an educational connivance becomes possible between students and staff which may give a wholly false emphasis to the importance of structured education. There is a good sense in which any designer worth the name will be a student for the whole of his working life. This is not only a function of creative resource, but also of the conditions of rapid technological change which a designer must meet in his work. In such a perspective, the few years in a design school are not unimportant, but should be carefully guarded against inflated claims for 'completing' the education of a designer. At best, three – or even five – years in design school can attend (thoroughly) to a few simple priorities in a designer's personal education. Even at a mundane level, much of what is called 'operational know-how' is necessarily picked up in the rub of professional practice.

What, then, is the special usefulness of a formal design education? Numbers of staff and students are gathered together in one place with a common purpose and common facilities. Students learn a great deal from each other; not only from books or from their tutors' guidance. These facts point to the benefits of academic life:

25

a gradually widening area of agreement (the norms against which individuality becomes meaningful), the experience of sharing, co-operating, and resolving conflicts: in a word, the chance of participation in all the stress and stimulus of a particular community with shared aims. This side of 'further education' is no less formative than the acquisition of skills and knowledge, much of which (not all) is equally available to the student who teaches himself from books, correspondence courses, or from the hard lessons of practical experience as an apprentice or design office assistant. The reality factors in academic life may appear to derive less from studio project work, which is always imperfectly 'real', than from the discussion that surrounds such work, the exploration of angles of attack, and the slow take-up represented by the experience of community.

Design education *must*, by its nature, dig below the surface, and must at the outset be more concerned to clarify intentions than to get results. If it is sensible to see learning and understanding as rooted in the continuum of life, it may be that a really useful introductory course will only show its value in the full context of subsequent experience; i.e. several years afterwards. Conversely, an education that concentrates on short-term results may give a misleading sense of achievement and fail to provide an adequate foundation for subsequent growth. This is a thorny problem, because under the pressurized and success-conscious conditions in which we live, students are naturally anxious to prove themselves as rapidly as possible (to themselves and their contemporaries and teachers). Something as intangible as the growth of understanding may seem a poor substitute for the almost measurable achievement marked by a high output of design projects, however specious or thinly considered such projects may be.

Degree or diploma work is a serious business for students, and can cause a great deal of anxiety, particularly to those who have a (perhaps well-founded) dread of examinations in any form. If such students will realize that their school work is but an intensive phase of a very lengthy design education, perhaps they will feel less undermined by those pressures. The purpose of coming to a design school is not, primarily, to gain a first-class degree, but to make a constructive use of several years' education. Some students, on the other hand, will find the edgy business of first- and second-class degree a positive stimulus or a useful objective to work toward. This is a matter of individual psychology: in a good school the course work should be rewarding enough to keep such matters in a tolerably angst-free perspective. An intelligent design course will also recognize that much design work is shared co-operative effort: students will be encouraged to help each other. In such matters it is sometimes necessary to educate the educators. A small-minded and uptight view of human experience will take small differences of accomplishment very seriously. A more generous view will allow that we are all holding candles in the dark.

Teachers who are practising designers may also have problems, by coming to feel that they have 'lost' ideas that may have cost them years of work, given and assimilated instantly and almost unnoticeably in the ordinary way of teaching exchanges; only to meet years afterwards the reproach that they have exploited their students' ideas to their own advantage. As designers well know, there is a private notebook of the mind stocked with ideas in various stages of development, and it is these that seem to disappear into teaching situations – rarely, in the nature of things, emerging in the form to which the designer's greater experience would have brought them. The origin of these occurrences is soon forgotten, but if a designer is teaching for any long length of time, he may feel increasingly deprived of his own creative identity. Such difficulties become obsessive only in overstructured teaching and learning relationships, where the us-and-them structure seems to generate attitudes akin to property-hoarding. It may be said here that a good design teacher will try to help a student to think through problems at his own pace and at the level of his own attainment. Such a teacher will communicate both his areas of confidence and the limits of his own awareness, thus putting forward the fruits of experience in a spirit of positive uncertainty. In this discretion, and in this spirit, 'models' and 'constructs' may become acceptable and unrestricting – not to copy, but to examine the thinking behind them, and how this has worked out. Models may be verbal or material, and constructs will be artefacts of one sort or another. As to students and staff, Frederic Samson put the matter pithily (addressing students at the Royal College of Art): 'the main difference between us is that your ignorance is superficial but mine is profound'.

27

Unfortunately such remarks would hardly be well taken in some schools and training colleges: too much is implied, of the life of knowledge, and of knowledge of life. Yet the challenge of a fast-changing global view of life stretches the imagination like elastic; it is ever more necessary that experiences nearer home are tethered to credibility, as distinct from pretension. There can be no doubt that many institutions have become seriously overstructured for the job they have to do. In education and elsewhere, the grip of outworn forms may discourage new energies beyond the toleration threshold within which differences are normally met and resolved. The parties involved find themselves talking in different languages in the same tongue, but with radically conflicting assumptions. Such new energies may be quite unformed, supported less by argument than by exploratory behaviour as such, and may be reaching toward new insights along unfamiliar paths of social exploration. This is the genesis of the student demonstration or sit-in.

Sit-ins and other demonstrations can become merely fashionable, or may become as rigidly institutionalized as the conditions they affect to challenge or displace. However, it is short-sighted to regard these happenings as mindlessly destructive, when they way generate and focus an extraordinary energy of self-education, quite remote from the ostensible aims of 'protest'. Indeed it is possible for those who detest revolutions to see such actions as genuinely an attempt at social adaptation; that is, to conditions which more ordinary channels of expression are failing either to contain or to anticipate. (Traditional forces of reaction will doubtless learn to keep up with the times.) Certainly a husk of discarded usages is revealed on these occasions, and one that has failed to grow with the perceptions of an impatient minority. At worst, the reaction provoked is too violently defensive to promise more than deep disillusion to the revolutionaries. At best, an institution is jerked out of complacency into a new consciousness of its privileges, and, for the participants, there may be a deeply moving experience of those twin principles for human conduct – solidarity and reciprocity (all for one and one for all, and an active spirit of empathy in human relations). The result is not (as commonly supposed) a developing group hysteria, but may be a notable growth of self-knowledge and individuation.

It is reasonable to mistrust any theory of conduct which draws life from the presence of an external enemy (or the necessary creation of such). Yet there is a dangerous doublethink that permits violence and apathy to be institutionalized in society, whilst deploring the faculty that young people have for detecting humbug in their elders. The intelligent way to meet any promise of new life must be with gratitude untinged by cynicism. Given favourable conditions for experiment, then the worth and staying power of new ideas will swiftly demonstrate themselves. It is only remarkable that, in practice, official educational attitudes are so deeply resistant to change that in some places the water settled placidly over the disturbances of 1968 as though they never happened; change being too often substituted by expansion. Above all it is necessary to defend the notion, and the fact, of pluralism in education; against the ever-possible threat of some new, centrally directed, and paralysing orthodoxy. Taken as a prescriptive cure-all, with no awareness of local conditions, even a 'network' can become a cage of emptiness.

Formal education is now under attack for its own credibility. If the gap between technical capability and social imagination is to be bridged, or if that problem is even to be energetically appraised, education must lose much of its formality in pursuit of a new warmth and flexibility of outlook. This does not imply abandoning standards of intellectual discourse or of real attainment in any field: on the contrary, it is the only hope of their survival within the education system. Every single concept of structured education needs to be freshly seen and needs to be overhauled (and, where necessary, rebuilt) from first principles. Given the will, such principles are neither hard of access nor beyond the reach of agreement. The essential realization is that the informal truths are closest to sources of wisdom and creativity, and that experimentation at all levels is not a luxury, but a first need of this time: in our work, in our leisure, and in the precarious survival that we hope to make more secure for our children. In all such efforts, there will be failures again and again. It is important to recognize that there is an honourable difference between failure by default – doing nothing or not even recognizing what might be done – and failure in an effort to do something worthwhile. What we may conceive as a genuinely free school may be as elusive as a free society and prone to as many internal contradictions; yet freedom must remain the one permissible tyranny.

As for design, there are times when to say no is a constructive act; to say yes, *as a designer* looking to the future, is to join social commitment to a mastery of particulars. In education, all we can do is make good work possible, and be alert to its coming; never fooling ourselves that all good things come easily. To work well is to work with love. A hail of words, like rain in April, can do no more than keep the air sharp and sweet and the ground springy underfoot; and that is the best a formal design education can hope to do – relevantly.

4 What is good design?

The 'goodness' or 'rightness' of a design cannot easily be estimated outside a knowledge of its purpose, and sometimes also of its circumstantial background. This is no reason for timidity of judgement; a man must reserve his right to say 'I like that; to me it is beautiful and satisfying, and more so than that one over there that works so much better' – or, 'this is a good workmanlike solution, thank God it has no pretensions to Art'. Theoretically, a well-integrated design should come so naturally to eye and hand that neither of these comments will be called upon, but human nature isn't so simply natural and nor is human society. An optimum solution is possible where the conditions for verification can refer to absolutes; a daunting and illusory requirement in most design situations. On the other hand, a design can say to us 'here is a problem that is so well understood that it can be felt to be moving toward an optimum solution; the design is inclined in that direction'. This is designers' talk; the user of a product will not be too interested in the skill with which a designer has met his constraints. If a design is so well-wrought that overtones of meaning are present, so that the work can be experienced (optionally) at many different levels simultaneously, then it is a condition of organic design that the further harmonics must not clutter or deform a simple level of acceptability.

For the designer, good design is the generous and pertinent response to the full context of a design opportunity, whether large or small, and the quality of the outcome resides in a close and truthful correspondence between form and meaning. The meaning of a good garden spade is seen in its behaviour, that it performs well; in its look and feel, its strength and required durability; in a directness of address through the simple expression of its function. More complex objects, places, equipment, situations, may well exhibit less obvious dimensions of meaning – of which one may be the property of reference discussed elsewhere in this book. A design decision may prefer some determinant principle of action to a material outcome. As a social activity, the integrity of design work proceeds from the understanding that every decision by one human being on behalf of another has an implicit cultural history. Design is a field of concern, response, and enquiry, as often as decision and consequence. In this sense (also), good design can both do its job well and speak to us.

Every design product has two missing factors which give substance to abstraction: realization and use. These are the ghostly but intractable realities never to be forgotten when sitting at a drawing board. In a similar way, any discussion of design philosophy must never stray too far from nuts and bolts and catalogues and every kind of material exigency: a designer breathes life into these things by the quality of his decision-making. Thus his concern is truly 'the place of value in a world of facts' (see the book by Köhler of that name) and the outcome can (or should) be a form of discourse; but not a verbal one. His work can be said to deploy the resources of a language and be accessible to understanding through the non-verbal equivalents of intention, tone, sense, and structure (cf. I. A. Richards), but there are other and more directly functional levels of experience which – as has been said – must come to the hand with all the attributes of immediacy. Most of the time a designer finds it hard enough to do small things well. Any number of broader considerations must not distract him from that task, but rather enliven and give sanction to its meaning.

A product must not only be capable of realization through manufacture, but in its very nature must respect all the human and economic constraints that surround production and effective distribution. This may seem obvious in the case of product and communication design. Similarly, it is difficult properly to evaluate a building without some idea of the cost factors and the client's briefing. Difficult, but not impossible, because a clear design will generally manage to state its own terms of reference, unless disaster has intervened at some stage to distort the central intention of the work. There are many cases in which a good design will be discarded for reasons which seem arbitrary, perhaps to be replaced by some meretricious product with a better sales-potential. Again, a perfectly adequate design solution, the result of much care and imagination in its development, may never reach the public at all. In this respect the artisan designer may enjoy a freedom denied to the designer for mass production (though his economic problems will limit the scale of the work), and much experimentation in form-giving will necessarily occur in situations exempt from marketing difficulties. These will include one-off jobs, limited production runs, and public work (schools, hospitals, airports, for example). Much early discussion in the modern movement assumed – broadly for social reasons – that product design (mass production for the consumer market) was the centre of inertia that had to be revitalized: Herbert Read's book *Art and industry* reflected this assumption in the 1930s. Gropius's *New architecture and the Bauhaus* contained a classical statement which seemed to imply that product design would move inexorably toward the 'type-form' for the problem examined.

As things have turned out, the most interesting work has happened, of course, where it was economically possible. The domestic consumer market has gained an important component in DIY (do-it-yourself) which in itself demands a reappraisal of the designer's role in the areas affected. The mass production of building or service components (such as pressed-out or moulded bathroom service units) has hardly approached the potential seen for it fifty years ago. The notion of 'place' as the focus for communal achievement has scarcely fought off the demands of 'occasion' and mobility, despite moving and articulate pleas from Aldo van Eyck and others – and despite the continuing reality of place as a factor of ordinary experience, eroded as it is by communications, and the rarity of imaginative work in this field. It is a mistake to see the designer's work as conjuring up new worlds at the scratch of a drawing pen: there are many fields in which the designer could profitably work with (for instance) do-it-yourself and co-operative housing agencies; and there are fields in which a designer can and should respect the organic continuity that surrounds people's lives. Two examples: the interior designer is doubtful of his 'responsibility' because everyone knows that architects should design their buildings from the inside outwards. In fact, there are plenty of buildings that are simply weather-proofed and service-provided shells, waiting for specific uses to be provided for. However, leaving that aside, it is not a necessary argument to suppose that given adequate social resources – the whole of our physical environment should be uprooted and totally replaced at regular intervals. This is a dangerous fantasy. In fact there is plenty of scope for the adaptation of existing buildings to new uses (a so-called slum area is as much a pattern of relationships as of decayed buildings) and this is interpretive work for which the 'interior designer' could be well-fitted. Again, there are plenty of structurally sound buildings that could be given extended life with the aid of a loan and a do-it-yourself handbook. As it is, the lunacy of high-rise development has only recently been seriously questioned; in practice, land values give rise to extraordinary palaces for paper-work springing out of areas of private squalor, and the simple things – like the provision of neighbourhood amenities – are neglected in favour of drawing-board schemes which may seriously debilitate the life that 'squalor' sometimes reflects. A run-down neighbourhood may need a lot of things but the problem must be seen in more than a tidy-minded way; every problem, however complicated by planning and growth statistics, is met with concealed assumptions (and often concealed economics). Here is ground both for humility and for diagnostic sensitivity in the way a designer approaches his work.

The difficulties for product designers are not just a matter of plain villainy on the part of manufacturers; they are, in part, a consequence of capitalism. Whilst strange things do go on in board-rooms, it must be realized that a well-designed product must be sold competitively. Experimental work may be chancy as a sales proposition. As things are, a first duty of a company director is to make his company profitable (which he may conceive as a first duty to his shareholders), and a second duty is to keep his work-people in continuous employment. Experiment becomes a closely calculated risk, very much at the mercy of the buyers in the retail trades, and subsequently dependent on a successful advertising policy, public response, and many other factors. In the furniture trade there are a few companies who have tried to maintain reasonable design standards, against the hope of improving them as the market 'softens' sufficiently to warrant further advancement. Such companies have relied on contract work furniture – for public buildings specified by architects or local authorities – to help carry them forward. It will be seen, at least, that under ordinary production conditions, product design cannot easily be evaluated against absolute standards, yet products meet constant criticism on such terms.

Unfortunately, it is also true that there are innumerable products that are just very poor realizations of a straightforward and entirely non-experimental design concept. They could have been marketed just as easily had they been designed with more distinction. The design capability simply was not there. Designers should be aware of property-relations as a conditioning factor in the way they design (and think about design), but no designer should fool himself that given 'a better society' it would then be magically easy to design well. A designer who stops designing in the hope of better things may lose his ability to design anything at all; to this extent people become what they do. Here, an idealistic student might consider the partial truth in the saying 'a few are artists, the rest earn a living' – which in caricature might be said of every profession and not less of the sciences than the arts. Those who elect to put their work before everything else, which is merely one of the conditions for complete mastery in any field, must fairly expect life to present some difficulties.

The hard facts of a market economy are easy to overlook in the relatively permissive ambience of the average art or design school. Although academic life is subject to its own peculiar stresses, economic sanctions are not pre-eminent among them. Fortunately, students need not harden themselves against a perpetual winter of creative frustrations: the situation is not as depressing as some of these remarks might suggest. It is true that a designer's freedom will reflect in large measure the values of the society in which he works. Designers are not privileged to opt out of the conditions of their culture, but *are* privileged to do something about it. The designer's training equips him to act for the community, as (in limited respects) the trained eyes and hands and consciousness of that community – not in some superior human capacity, but in virtue of the perceptions which he inherits from the past, embodies in the present, and carries forward into the future. He is of and for the people; and for them, and for himself, he must work at the limit of what he sees to be good. The sentimentality of talking down, or working down, is a waste of the social energies invested in his training: thus can 'social realism' enshrine the second-rate.

If society is geared to satisfactions on the cheap, the designer has a special responsibility to straighten himself out in that respect;

to decide where he stands. When real needs are neglected, and arti-
ficial ones everywhere stimulated into an avid hunger for novelty,
sensation, and status-appeal, largely (but not wholly) for reasons
of private or public profit; then here is his own nature, his own
society. He is involved, and he must decide how best to act. It should
not surprise him to find a thin and pretentious reality informing
the design language of the world which he inherits. A Marxist (or
anarchist) analysis may be one tool to help him sort this out, but
he will hardly need to put on Marxist spectacles to see that a veneer
of good taste has 'reference' to certain obvious social conditions
and is not the whole of good design. The design student may sometimes find that the industrial scrap-heaps, the surplus stores, and
the products of straightforward engineering, will yield images of
greater vitality than will be found in more fashionable quarters
(though even here, fashion spies out the land). Such a situation is a
challenge, and as such must be studied and understood.

Yet it is still no answer to live in the future; every skill must be
nurtured by a commitment in depth to the present. The meaning
of creativity may be seen as an equation which resolves this apparent paradox. Work that lives is rooted in the conditions of its time,
but such conditions include awareness, dreams, and aspirations, as
much as the resources of a specific technology: such work respects
the past and actually creates the future. These problems, and their
wider implications for human happiness, will necessarily concern
students of design, because no one can make truly creative decisions without understanding; and without a real participation in
the constructive spirit of his time. *This spirit must be sought out*,
not necessarily by intellectual means, to be honoured wherever it
is found.

Those who are depressed by the shoddiness of our environment
(except in those areas of economic privilege where it is customary to
buy up the past), should study the spirit of the modern movement
in its development from the turn of the century to the late 1930s.
Here they will find themselves in good and most various company.
As Walter Gropius often explained, the modern movement was not
some matter of dogma, fashion, or taste, but a profoundly wide-
ranging attempt to encompass the nature of the twentieth-century
experience and to meet its physical demands with a constructive
response.

What may excite us mostly about this phenomenon is its surface appeal, the tangible achievement; a whole world of very explicit imagery conjured, as it must now seem, out of nothing – an entirely fresh start. The fact of conditions historically different from our own does not diminish the marvel of this achievement and its continuing relevance. This has nothing to do with imitating the forms of the past (near or distant): anyone who sees the modern movement in stylistic terms will fail to understand its radical nature. It is also necessary to accept that most work of today (meaning 'modern' or 'contemporary') is an enfeebled and misunderstood derivation from this earlier work, almost wholly removed from its inspiration, its most deeply rooted concerns, and the force of its guiding spirit.

The effort of zero, of the 'tabula rasa', of the new beginning, is not in principle a stylistic option (though in retrospect it may be so viewed); it is an effort consequent upon certain perceptions, for which, obviously, there will be equivalents in prophetic or diagnostic acumen, across a whole civilization experiencing radical change – or perhaps it is truer to say, waking up to a foreshortened view of what such change might seem to imply. Earlier models, and the canons of idle change, the sports of fancy, become suddenly and drastically inadequate. The call is certainly to 'clear from the head the masses of impressive rubbish' and to 'make action urgent and its nature clear'; it is also to 'look shining at / New styles of architecture, a change of heart' (the quotations are from the poet Auden of the 1930s) but most of all it is an effort of address toward the irreducible; that modest yet most demanding of entitlements. Is there indeed any alternative? but silence; as George Steiner has remarked in another context. The possibly prophetic nature of such insights is often overlooked, especially when accusing the modern movement of a false and shallow optimism; as though a culture of utility could not be expected to ask 'what is it decently possible to assert, given the claustrophobic banality of a present, and the seeming threat of a future?' Less, perhaps, an insight than an indistinct awareness, and one of two negative imperatives at work, the other being *the need to stop telling lies*.

What more active principles are involved (or indeed, derived). It is usual to account for the modern-ness of modern work in terms of influences and precedents, the technological and social pressures, new materials and techniques, the convergent history of ideas, and so forth. It is obvious that orders of form, and forms of order, are design specifics in a practical way and experienced concretely, not as a set of abstracted verbal propositions. Yet as Viktor Frankl points out, in his book written from direct experience of the concentration camps, it is curiously easy to overlook, in any analysis of human motivation, the tenacious strength of the human search for meaning. It is here that the irreducible, the without-which-not, the minimal, the verification principle, 'truth to materials', and the notion of accountability, have their roots. At a different level, it is fairly obvious that failing the imitation of natural form (the dead-end of art nouveau), a verification principle would move towards number and geometry stripped of backward reference or depleted symbolism. 'Clear expression', no unseen props, and the most for the least (the strengthening of signal and the reduction of noise) have to be seen as necessary correlates to any search from zero for significant form – given a situation of survival, as distinct from options consulted on a broad wave of optimism concerning human progress.

However, it was the second broad outreach of the modern movement, involving nine more positive principles as guides to action (in fact there are a few more), that rescued a search for meaning from being merely the celebration of a rather unattractive rectitude. These are the social principles – not unwarrantably, design being a transactional art – and they prefigure certain changes in human relations which have not occurred, but may well have to if our society is to become less death-orientated. It is in this sense that the modern movement might be said to be prefigurative, and in this sense that its effort was betrayed (forgotten) in the take-over by the complicated apparatus of commercialism. These principles may be briefly stated as follows.

The first principle is that of self-determination: the search for a subset of self-generative principles within the situation as found; as expressed by the saying 'a well stated problem is more than half solved' and, as suggested elsewhere in this book, 'a designer transforms constraint into opportunity'. As things get under way, the principle enables the job to speak up for itself with increasing confidence and fluency. Sometimes this is falsely seen, so that in fact a designer able enough to work in this way is not actually being instructed by the job, so much as providing a good fit (i.e. just being a good designer); the imposition of arbitrary form always throws up a lot of noise and is in other ways more conspicuous. However, it is interesting that this principle, which applies very well in a straight designer-client relationship, is also flexible enough to accommodate quite different design attitudes, including those that might be thought anti-design by those who see the modern movement in formal terms (see part 7 for a discussion of this matter).

The second principle is that of reasonable assent; that what is done should be essentially coherent, intelligible, and open to discussion. (There are problems of language here which will not detain us: from the standpoint of principle, which becomes 'generative' to the way something is done, the fuel of continuing intention is more important than the ash of dead fires.)

The third is that every part in a job should work for its living ('From each according ...'). This implies distinction and emphasis not from privilege', or prior status, but from functional differentiation within the whole. This principle (aided by others) entails asymmetry, a clear structure, and certain negative imperatives mentioned earlier. (For example, in a chair, the absence of glued blocks reinforcing an unsound structural principle, or, alternatively, a structure no longer covert, but derived from glued blocks.)

The fourth principle is that objects should be designed as well as possible for use and not for profit; and that where an object cannot be designed at all unless by definition it is profitable, then the resulting compromise is against principle and not with it. The modern movement has (rightly) been accused of political naïvety by supposing that optimized design was conceivable in mass production, where marketing arrangements will ensure a good product being swept away to stimulate fresh demand. Anyone who wishes to see such matters imaginatively explored should read E.C. Large's novel *Sugar in the air*.

The fifth principle is that of anonymity; poignantly expressed in the effort to mass-produce objects of quality at low prices; more adventitiously, and sometimes trendily, in the way that designers like the idea of their Thonet chairs, jeans, clothes-pegs – not to mention the universal boot. The requirement in either case is that the particular should be seen as a special case of an available universal. The principle is also, implicitly, an attack upon the art-object so constituted by its scarcity value (for discussions of which, see John Berger's writings). An extended requirement is the suppression of unwarranted detail (which in turn entails a special case of the third principle, namely that elements are distinguished from components), such that the fuss of idiosyncrasy slips below conscious regard. The human being is thus freed to enjoy a 'true' idiosyncrasy, supposedly more authentic in being less object-fixated; so that what was once merely idiosyncratic becomes genuinely individual. Thus by discovering what is uniquely true to himself (as distinct from conferred status) the road is open to self-transcendence. (See Buber's *The way of man* for a poetic uncovering of this theme.) At a less difficult level, the principle finds expression in an allegiance to the 'set' or series (of knives, of wine glasses, or whatever) in preference to the unique and single object. The attentive reader will have noted that this principle is the most vulnerable, the most open to corruption, and the most liable to misunderstanding (old ladies deprived of their tea-cosies and sentimental possessions, reds under the bed).

The sixth principle expresses a deep desire for a new vernacular (grown out of the alienation we all feel) – seeking articulation in a popular, indigenous, locally based, and relatively unselfconscious design language; adding a sense of place to that of space, of repose and location as a counter to mobility, and so on. Less wistfully, the principle develops an interest in the simple and functionally-derived design solution, often with engineering overtones (cf. canal buildings and structures, barns, windmills, and small houses everywhere pre-1850). Local variants are usually involved – of materials and technique – and there is a predilection for small or controllable human scale. This principle has always run strongly as a current of inspiration in the modern movement, but in the early years found expression as its apparent opposite (i.e. as a paradox), namely, as an implacable resistance to sentimental craft-revivals and every other evidence of a falsely imposed vernacular: the conviction that there are no short cuts to Elysium except through 'the assimilated lessons of the machine' (a view characteristically developed by Lewis Mumford in *Technics and civilization*). The way back is seen to be through faith and through the wilderness, and a refusal to be conned by snap answers (e.g. the candles and leathers syndrome). It is interesting, of course, that some of this antipathy can be traced to the parentage of the modern movement in the arts and crafts, and that now the movement is finding it easier to come to terms with its parents in the realm of the Alternative (see part 6), the principle is gaining confidence; it is no longer so wilfully 'protecting the lost wisdom of the tribe' behind the fortifications of an arrogant modernism. However, it should be clear how the modern movement has come to be misunderstood on this point. Who was it who said that the true romantics of this age would be its most ardent classicists? I shall not waste time on the ignorant supposition that the modern movement is about high-rise buildings (or ever was, intrinsically).

The seventh principle is possibly the most important (though this is too puffed-out a word – formative is better) and it is the most closely linked to insights available from other areas of our culture: it is, of course, the search for relationship as distinct from self-sufficiency, or self-containedness, and everything that this might be held to imply at every level of decision in design. This includes, and perhaps most prominently, the complex realm of formal relationships, and how once this principle is grasped – an entirely new way of working is disconcertingly revealed. If you had to explain to your aunt just what it is that makes 'typically modern design' different in kind to any other, this is the single principle that you would have to invoke. It is thus at once a principle of search, of reference, and of explication. Something of this is discussed in part 5 and elsewhere.

The eighth is the existential principle: that *there shall be nothing else*; and that what there is, shall be contingently respected. This most elusive of principles, is at the same time the most down-to-earth. From its employ springs the ad hoc, the improvised, the antiinstitutionalized; and on the other hand, a healthy disrespect for the tyranny of absolutes. The joker in the pack.

Finally, the ninth principle (appropriately, that of the dance) is the translation of mass into energy and relationship. It is, in a sense, the dancing out of the seventh. This principle does not go as far as Proudhon ('property is theft') though it shakes the old boy warmly by the hand somewhere along the line; nor does it foolishly believe that the silicon chip will free mankind of its material adhesions; it is, however, the energetic principle, and as such must be assumed to be always embryonic with the hope of new life. It is also, of course, if you care to follow through Illich's indications, a holy celebrant. There are three lesser, facilitating principles – including that concerned with standard and standardization – but they will not be discussed here.

Now; if 'design' is overlooked and the preceding paragraphs reconsidered as metaphor, it should be clear that the nine principles translate very potently into the prerequisites for an apolitical social revolution, and that this is no accident. It might also follow that a constructive art – design – can have, does have, an intelligibly expressive content. Of the two sets of ideas here, the first of which I described as 'negative imperatives', it could be said that the first collapse into a single pinched-face-personal-probity-principle, doomed to emaciation and 'the distortions of ingrown virginity' without the saving social outreach of the nine, which (on this analogy) are self-transcending. Returning now to the modern movement, the correspondence should be clear. The principles are, of course, interdependent (and much simplified) – as in the theory of compass adjustment, you have to put everything back together again before it makes sense. However, it would be inadmissible to have this discussion at all, were it not for the fact that for every principle mentioned here (including the first sub-set) there are precise physical correlates to be found, in the field both of object design and of design procedure generally. The notion that the modern movement prefigured certain qualitative changes in our society whereby human survival might be the better assured (under the industrial challenge) is not, on this argument, as fanciful as it might otherwise appear. It is true that this book is written from a declared standpoint, and therefore discusses design (here) in an unorthodox way. It is also true, and one function of the discussion to demonstrate, that this movement can never usefully be seen as a fashionable option that now happens to be passé. It is a serious demand upon intellectual assent and practical action.

Something of this is well expressed by Paul Schuitema, the graphic designer who worked in the Netherlands and Germany in the 1920s and 1930s.

'We didn't see our work as art; we didn't see our work as making beautiful things. We discovered that the romantic insights were lies; that the whole world was suffering from phraseology; that it was necessary to start at the beginning. Our research was directed to finding new ways, to establishing new insights – to find out the real characteristics of tools and creative media. Their strengths in communication – their real value. No pretence, no outward show. Therefore, when we had to construct a chair or a table, we wanted to start with the constructive possibilities of wood, iron, leather and so on; to deal with the real functions of a chair, a living room, a house, a city: social organization. The human functions. Therefore, we worked hand-in-hand with carpenters, architects, printers, and manufacturers.

To reduce chaos to order, to put order into things. To make things more clear, to understand the reasons. It was the result of social movement. It was not a fashion or a special view of art. We tried to establish our connection with the social situation in our work … The answer to our problems must be the questions: why? what for? how? and with what?'

The attractive qualities of this statement should not blind us to the fact that the modern movement has always been a minority struggle, carried on against a good deal of practical opposition, and, at best, a widely felt social indifference. At least in its early days the conflict was capable of clear definition.

It is necessary to stress some of the background considerations which prompted modern design into being, because it is too easy to study the designs that emerged as specially privileged historical

43

monuments, whereas the spirit that conceived them is still alive and accessible to us. In forming our own criteria for 'good' design, we cannot, of course, escape the half-conscious assumptions which make us always the children of our own time, but we do well to remember that our own concerns are in some respects closer to the years between the two world wars than to the world of the 1950s. A whole complex of emergent ideas, values, and experimental work was traumatically cut short by the experience of fascism, the horrors of Auschwitz and Hiroshima, and by the slow aftermath of cultural assimilation. Not only were energies dispersed in a practical way, but their foundations were uprooted. The implicit philosophy which underpinned modern design was never very far from what is wearily referred to as 'a rational view of man's conduct': the hope and even the confidence that if technology could only be integrated into meaningful value-structures, a new and fruitful way of life lay open to man's willing acceptance. The Second World War brutally damaged that hope.

For those who see the world as essentially an arena of conflict between good and evil, however, there can surely be no doubt that the modern movement stands for clarity, sweetness, and light; order, relation, and harmony; made accessible through the only means that are fully credible to our experience of this time. To open up a new age of revival or pastiche (the weakest form of wit) is merely to admit defeat in this sector of creative possibilities. Defeat may seem inevitable, radical change may seem a prerequisite for confidence of any kind, perhaps our civilization really cannot survive on its own terms; any of these realizations (if accepted) carries a more appropriate response than backsliding into a weakly fashionable eclecticism.

It is certainly obvious that a rational view must examine motivational forces with a more intimate sense of their origins, and the cost of their frustration. In the design field it is not just a matter of exchanging affective imagery for austerities that are deemed to have had their day. Here pop must be distinguished from vernacular; the one being a brilliantly successful commercial racket and the other being an unavailable option except at a stylistic level (see Herbert Read's poem, part 7). Our civilization has refined many hells, but in the realm of voluntary srrvitude it would be hard to beat the inanity of pop music radio, with perhaps a few television commercials thrown in for good measure. A language of gesture and exclamation tends always toward infantilism; a measure of its warmth but also of its inadequacy. If a new synthesis of thought and feeling is to be attempted, we must think and feel our way toward the place of design in a necessary context of social renewal. Nor must we forget that a warm heart and a rather special view of history do not make a designer. Designing is very specific; a cultivated understanding is no guarantee of a specific creativity. This is the individual problem and a central concern of this book. For the social task we have fresh evidence all the time of man's fallibility, of his deepening technological commitment; of the nature of affluence divorced from social or spiritual awareness. Yet there is a pedantry of the spirit in dwelling too much on these things. The force of new life can break through where and when we least expect it; as in Paris in May 1968, when the impossible seemed suddenly within reach.

It should at least be clear that to speak of 'good' design is to speak of, and from, the conditions of our own time, and our response to these conditions. The intelligibility – and perhaps the existence – of a design 'language' is a problem of the cultural fragmentation that affects participation in every other aspect of our culture. Because the realization of a designer's work is always socially contingent, his freedoms are always a recognition of necessity in a most explicit way. An elegant design solution is one that meets all the apparent conditions with a pleasing economy of means. A fruitful solution co-opts the conditions into a new integration of meaning, whereby what was 'apparent' is seen to have been insufficient. Such answers have questions in them.

5   Problems with method

The case for analytical technique – of the simplest order – rests on the premise that you should find out what you are doing, or what you should be doing, before considering how to do it; and that this degree of foresight is normal to the role and situation of a designer. Such a claim is not unreasonable. In medical terms, for instance, a prescription will be a very hit-and-miss affair unless there has been a diagnosis; and in converting a building, a drawn plan will be rather vague unless it has been converted from an accurate survey. In either case there are known procedures, and techniques, that will help to avoid wasted time and effort. So much is very nearly self-evident. Methodology goes further, by suggesting that preferred models are available for the definition of goals and the allocation of effort, and that if they are correctly employed, the designer's work can be guided towards an optimum solution that might otherwise have eluded him, except through the mediation of happy accident.

This is a somewhat crass simplification of the methodological position, and indeed to discuss it at all is to invite simplification; partly to keep clear of the dead language that the subject seems to attract, and partly to sidestep the quicksands of theory and debate that surround problem-solving and methodology, keeping most de-signers thoughtfully at a distance. This is a partly abandoned terri-tory, and strewn with old workings – though there is life in some of them yet. Apart from the remaining devotees, who work out of sight and occasionally surface with new formulations, there are always small bands of students, picking over the discarded hopes and new offerings. The idea that the myth of creativity can be domesticated, and perhaps told how to behave – in terms at once 'scientific' and 'verifiable' – seems always to fascinate those who feel somehow de-nied by the myth, or outside its provenance. Jung speaks of the alchemists in this context, and the matter is discussed exhaustively (for ordinary mortals) in Arthur Koestler's *The act of creation*, a work that could usefully head the more specialized book references in the field, but rarely does. After all, Koestler wrote that fine novel

Darkness at noon, which helps to argue for his credibility as a guide.

However, if there are real dangers in taking methodology and problem-solving too seriously, the supposed freedoms available from randomly 'intuitive' approaches are notoriously treacherous when the work is technically and functionally complex or demanding. Unless properly guided by diagnostic technique the outcome will tend to lack both objectivity and depth of thought, and in failing to break through invisible cordons of mental sets and prior assumptions, can become little more than a thinly rationalized ego-projection. It can also be said for methodology that in an often crooked way, its heart is in the right place. Even if a mouse-like issue is the result of seemingly elephantine labours, and even if in the process, a simple opportunity is mistaken for a 'problem', at least the effort is properly outward-looking; an effort of service. The other way of looking at it is to go back to part 1 and simply say that procedures appropriate to designing textiles will hardly do for the design of an operating theatre. Fortunately the breadth of the design spectrum is very accommodating, not only to a variety of opportunities, but to many different kinds of person. This part will inspect a few small-scale design situations to see how they look, and how they measure up; only thus will the relevant design attitudes fall into place, and seem less abstract in discussion.

Let us begin with chair design – although small in scale, one of the most difficult of design assignments. I remember discussing this with a Danish architect. He said that after ten years practice he felt he should be ready to try designing a chair. It was a failure. Now, five years later, he felt he was further along his road and perhaps it was time to have another go. Of course, if you are making something to please yourself, you can freely set your own terms of reference (as perhaps this designer was doing). This will not make things easier than working to a commission; merely different. You can decide, for instance, if it takes you that way, to make a chair the function of which is to question the notion of comfort, and which is therefore designedly uncomfortable to the point of actually collapsing when sat in. (A 'sign for sitting' with question mark added.) This may not be as daft as it sounds. Designers get accustomed to the support of many constraints (limiting conditions) in the way they normally work. Remove these and it is like putting an engine out of gear suddenly, it returns to idling speed, or feels purposeless when accelerated. One way to get the measure of a job, and to get close to it, is to project its life to absurdity (in all directions: scale, function, material, etc.) and then to pull back to some sense of boundary in what you propose to do. This technique is useful in many design situations. It was illustrated for me by a marvellous musician and a great teacher (Niso Ticciati) from whom I once had the privilege of some cello lessons. He said I should always try to form a mental picture of the whole arc of traverse of which the body, arm, and bow movement, were capable. When the bow then engaged a string briefly, for a short distance, to form a musical note – and given enough practice – the sound would come to be full and free and true. If on the other hand I approached with a picture or 'Gestalt' of just the right size, and length of contact between bow and string, and therefore unconsciously aimed for that, the sound would be tight, thin, and restricted. He put it much better. The principle is worth dwelling upon in the imagination; it has many applications.

Suppose alternatively that a designer is commissioned to design (say) a polypropylene chair for factory production. The designer (you) will be involved in an intricate investigation of the possible – in terms of marketing, costs, production techniques, user requirements – that will compel you to conduct research in a fairly methodical way. You will be acting as an agent in a social transaction involving other people's lives and jobs and interests. It will certainly help to have guidelines for your own allocation of time and energy. The form of the chair – assuming 'normal' standards of comfort – will be to some extent preconditioned by what you find out about the human body, and where and how the chair might be used. Materials and form will be impinged upon by structural and other performance considerations, some of which may not be revealed except after the prolonged testing of a prototype, and also by the costs of tooling up for the job. The chair may be part of a 'set'; some grouping of furniture intended (now or in the future) to go together, in which case you will have to devise a formal vocabulary that will fit all cases (if loosely). The job would not be untypical of product design for a retail market. Such work involves a high degree of generality – the highest common denominators of everybody's needs, as interpreted by the buyers' estimate of market demand. (The 'buyer' is the person in the retail trade who places the orders.)

A simple problem analysis would help you with this job, and would net for you, for instance, the required life of the chair as a genuine condition to first question and subsequently work with. However, the scale and nature of the work would hardly demand more analysis than would come naturally as a refinement of common sense. Your real difficulty would be in satisfying the required conditions, having established what they are, and then designing what you felt to be a good chair out of those conditions. It could turn out that just one condition was paramount. To bring this factor into the light, you might well employ some of the techniques discussed further on in this book. More likely, however, 'good' for you would have to be defined as an educated designer's appreciation of chair-form nicely realized out of all the limiting conditions, one of which would be its acceptability to a less design-educated public. Tooling costs might be so heavy that you would have to be sure about this. On the other hand, you would not be asked to exercise unsupported judgement on issues outside your competence; if anything, your competence may be underestimated if you fail to ask searching and intelligent questions right at the outset. Here is a fairly tight situation for a designer; his margins of freedom are tightly drawn. All the more reason to find out how many of the apparent restrictions are real, inevitable; and how many merely reflect the habits and prejudices of your employer.

This could become acutely relevant in any design job outside the special conditions that attend product design. Building design, or say the interior design of some public space might offer you far more latitude for responsible decision. Suppose your client has asked for chairs but your analysis of the situation suggests that chairs are quite unnecessary – the needs of this area have been wrongly seen. Here it will be the seating *situation* that you examine. It is always a designer's job to hold in mind two counter-propositions: in this case, the particular notion of 'chair', as against the general notion of 'sitting' – only by departing from the familiar and particular case, can the designer freshly appraise its context and meaning; returning, perhaps, with a modified view of 'chair', or perhaps something quite different. New relationships may have emerged which alter the terms of the argument.

Drawing again upon personal experience, I was once asked to

refurnish such a public area in a much used part of a college build-ing. The area was noisy and unattractive and the existing furniture was badly knocked about. It soon became clear that if people were sitting down at all it was almost certainly in the wrong place and in the worst conditions for their comfort. By observation and question-ing and taking opinions it began to emerge that this furnishing difficulty was merely symptomatic of problems that were located elsewhere. It was necessary not only to trace the circulation habits and patterns through this part of the building, but to ask more basic questions. In the end – and to cut a long story short – the whole area was replanned to include new student common rooms, recep-tion rooms for guests, a public information area, a coffee-bar, and various other provisions. This in turn required the whole college to be reappraised in the light of long-term proposals for improving staff-student relationships so far as they were affected by physical environment. This required considerable alterations to offices, en-trances, and other facilities. The proposals, and all the reasons sup-porting them, were sent out in report form to the various interests involved, and as may be imagined, much discussion took place be-fore the scale of the problems, and their unfamiliarity, became gen-erally recognized. In this case a problem analysis has begun with a small and apparently self-contained problem, but has finally so changed its terms of reference that 'chairs' have long since disap-peared from detailed consideration (though at some point seating design will resurface as a practical design opportunity). Not only has the job become larger, but different in kind; questions of hu-man needs and human behaviour have taken over from structural or material or aesthetic preoccupations (to return, of course, in new permutations).

Before leaving this example it is worth adding that if the client or the community as a whole had rejected the proposals, or been unable to afford them, it would still have been right to place any temporary action within a future perspective, and within a broad examination of the present. No use (on this argument) just treating a symptom. Yet there are limits to the 'broad view' – even cost limits – and there are also dangers attached to it. As with leaders or even dictators – one in ten may be benign, compassionate, and construc-tive, whereas the rest may be hell. The designer with the Napoleonic vision may actually be rather a bad designer, however correct his analysis. Here the attractions of a piecemeal solution become evident, and recall those of medicine as against surgery; as is said of the surgeons, they love their work too well. And surgery can go wrong.

There are, of course, alternatives. The designer might recommend a series of happenings or improvisations that would be in constant change, thus passing the buck to one form of participatory decision-making. He would not be designing any 'thing' as such, but recommending and arguing for the course of action that seemed most appropriate, and that would continue to pose the problem rather than answer it. Or he might suggest an interim solution; a set of more controlled experiments to see what can be done with the spaces, thus gradually accumulating evidence for a more far-reaching and a more structured solution at some time in the future. By this means the constants in the situation would become gradually manifest constants, mostly, of behaviour and expectation – and the variables could be left to look after themselves. This is a bit like leaving a much-used swing door without a finger plate, in order to see what pattern of finger-marking builds up, before deciding what to do about it. A third alternative is quite common – to system-build from commercially available kits of parts, which can be dismantled and rebuilt or adjusted at will. This most reticent of alternatives (or cop-outs, as some designers might think) is seemingly in the customers' best interests. However, in practice, the most 'flexible' solutions, theoretically at the free disposal of the user, can come to feel either denuded of life, or psychologically tyrannous (or both); while an apparently rigid and very definite organization of a space can bestow freedom.

It is like living with all one's furniture (and maybe house as well) made out of perforated metal section; there is a continuous subliminal suggestion that you might be missing out on some better permutation of the parts. For qualities of definiteness in environments, it is worth examining some of the hill towns in Italy. The freedom bestowed by a walled town is – like some systems of belief – protectively finite; it is also that of recognition (by territorial boundaries, a most animal requirement). Presupposed, however, is a sense of necessity, of belonging, of history (therefore, of implied

51

continuity into a future), and of an aggregate slowly cohering into what is finally experienced as an organic whole. It is a mistake to think that vernacular can be turned on at will, as a formal option; or made in any way easily at all, when in fact it is grown; but the study of vernacular form is more than a consolation of philosophy, it is a source of joy to the spirit and the senses. Our own situation is closer to 'seek simplicity and mistrust it'. A brand new office block is no match for such assets, however well designed. In part (but not, alas, in whole) this failing is a function of the papery and repetitious purposes that such buildings must serve – and thus, of a society that deploys its energies so barrenly. There are (incidentally) a few meliorist tactics for the softening of hard architecture, discussed by Robert Sommer in his book *Tight spaces*.

Turning to lighter stuff, there are some forms of display and exhibition design so volatile, colourful, and impermanent, that anything so ponderous as 'analysis' would strike them stone dead. This is the realm of theatre and the market place. An exhibition stand of this kind often succeeds or fails by the 'élan vital' of a single overriding idea, to which everything else is strictly subordinate. The 'idea', however, will still have to be proposed, defended, found feasible, and – worst of all – realized. It is one thing to have a brilliant idea, quite another to make it work. Thus even here, a designer will find that he is not exempt from a good deal of hard thinking and from all the communication and other techniques that forward, prompt, order, and regulate, such thinking. As is well known (or should be), if an argument persuades by its simplicity, usually someone has done their homework: the most economical design may conceal the most arduous preparation. Other and more sober forms of exhibition design (museum display is an example) are normally quite outside the possibility of improvisation, and need a most carefully balanced appraisal of every factor relevant to the design. Exhibitions with a mainly informative content may sometimes go to extreme limits just to avoid being dull, and therefore non-communicative. Such weighting is well within the middle-spectrum range of ordinary design problems. It remains true, however, that exhibition design generally is wide-latitude design; often enough it gets away with little more than a well-acted conviction of purpose.

Graphic designers very often begin with a false brief from their client which will need to be taken right back to its origins before design (in the ordinary sense) can begin. This applies less to bookwork than to the very wide field in which designers are now employed. Exhibition design is an example. The graphic designer may have full responsibility, employing another designer with structural competence as an assistant or collaborator; or the roles may be reversed. Either way a root concept will have to be mutually understood and discussed, and the design may depart far from an initial briefing. Often there is a vagueness of function in exhibition design – the exhibitor may just want to 'be seen to be present' but in a favourable light; but may not put it (or see it) quite in that way. Whatever the requirements turn out to be, it is clear that the specialists involved must understand each other, and to do that they must speak the same language, at least up to the point where technical expertise begins to take over. Such examples point to the dubious logic of educating designers in compartments, and of over-using words like 'two-dimensional'. When was an exhibition ever a two-dimensional experience, or for that matter, catalogues, and other forms of jobbing graphics?

When design decisions are very open and unconstrained – and this might occur in any field of design, not merely in ceramics and textiles where it is usually assumed to occur – it is all the more necessary that the designer has some shared sense of context with other specialists. This need not imply one way or one culture, but does imply a history and a pedigree in any cultural effort. Nobody starts from nowhere; in which case it is better to determine your sources of inspiration, to go after them, and to try to understand what they are about. Otherwise a designer's vision is simply being programmed by 'the surface of the face of things'. It would be silly, for instance, to start designing modern fabrics intended for modern buildings with no understanding whatever of modern architecture. A true understanding involves more than a few images of interiors. It involves what has been attempted in the whole field of object-relations, and the questions, hopes, or assumptions that underpin modern design – that make it intelligible. The textile designer (or other specialist) who conceives the work as self-expression, and works solely with other like-minded specialists, may make or design some very nice things. In the long run, however, the work will be deprived of connection, of 'due weight' in its context of use, of appropriateness; it will tend to become, in short, self-contained. The opposite was true of some of the very subtle block-stripe curtain materials that used to come from Scandinavia; such material reaches out to its possible context and does not feel 'complete' without it – a property, partly, of directional flow but not peculiar to linear design.

Designing for a missing factor – that of use – is an interesting matter. It is continuously a problem in chair design, where too anatomically receptive a form will seem intrusively empty when nobody is sitting in it – which may mean for most of its life. Its immediate neighbours will be reinforcing the problem. This is one reason why Thonet chairs and stickbacks work so well spatially; they seem to comb space with just a sufficiently forward reminder of their existence. Space flows through them.

A much smaller and formally perfect example is the old Pelikan Graphos pen (as one now has to say, nib-holder) – always a joy to hold and to behold. This pen is a cylinder so pure that aficionados find ample variants in the doming of the ends (the radius of which can provoke discussion), the length of the pocket clip, which unaccountably varies, and the barely-visible placing of the maker's imprint. The clip is itself a 'tour de force' executed without break in the formal language. Here is fine-tolerance decision-making, though coarse by engineering standards, and it is against the severity of the cylinder that the user notes an appropriate weakening of one end, where a screw thread for the cap is turned. Thus only when the pen is used, and the cap duly screwed in place, is the integrity of the cylinder fully asserted. However the geometry is of course weakened at the business end where the nib is now revealed (nibs are individually inserted): the joy, of course, is the transference from formal language to active function, so that what might seem visually weak is suddenly felt as intelligently strong; a case of function compensating form. The fact that the pen works so well (though it is not easy to use, the two are not the same), in that it will produce with precision lines from quarter-inch thick to a hairline in equally precise gradations, provides a functional authority against which all these small points gain in the telling. However, the firm was taken over, the new version works just as well, employs the same principle, and has been 'restyled'. I say no more.

Here then are considerations of some subtlety whereby one design is found acceptable as against its functionally identical counterpart. In designing the pen in the first place, what 'procedures' or 'methods' would bring a designer towards such a distinction, help him to perceive it, and encourage the perception to become deeply felt? This is one thing to think about; the other is the scale and nature of the distinctions, and the power in them, once perceived.

In the general nature of formal disciplines, it is worth mentioning a common and vulgar heresy rife in some of the colleges, and sometimes supported with more vigour than understanding by Assessors, Course Validators, etc: it is to suppose that every design decision must of its nature demonstrate 'fresh and original thinking', and that the work must be coarse-grained – bear the marks of travail over a wide area of decision-making. This view is partly an unhappy legacy of the competitive spirit that we take for granted in secondary schooling, and which goes on to bedevil higher education in almost all its manifestations. Such thinking has much to do with the serious mismatch between education and 'real life' whenever the gladiatorial degree-taking image is confused with the conditions of design practice. However, these matters are less relevant here than one practical consequence, which is a confusion of gross with fine decision-making. The distinction may in fact be one of gross and subtle judgement.

To illustrate this the Pelikan must be exchanged for a bicycle. As will be seen, the two objects have something in common, at least in the context of this discussion. Consider the situation of a student working on the design of a bicycle. Now this machine is a beautifully tested and developed type-form over a given range of performance conditions; it is known to be a remarkably efficient energy-converter, and it is indubitably the product of a vast amount of co-operative human endeavour to get it to its present stage of refinement. Is there any good reason to redesign the bicycle from first principles? The answer must surely be – probably not, unless you posit quite new conditions of use to which the standard design is ill-adapted. It might be argued that there are such conditions, such as the effects of parking and fuel problems on commuter traffic. Designers have addressed themselves once again to the folding portable bicycle, which commuters and others might take on public transport. The folding Bickerton with its carrying bag is one light-weight answer; a bit fiddly and doubtless the principle is capable of further development; other and more seemingly radical designs have been published, but not it seems yet marketed. The Bickerton uses conventional spoke wheels and other standard components; it is to that extent a compromise, perhaps, but it works well. There is an inevitable loss of efficiency once the machine is rolling, as compared with a full-size light-weight cycle; this has always been the case with small-wheeled machines and for good reasons. No doubt there will be further work on special purpose bicycles where rolling efficiency can be set against more compelling criteria.

However, the fact remains that within a developed type-form there is still a very great subtlety of possible variants and a considerable range for them. In the case of the bicycle, this applies not only to matters like the design of accessories to develop possible uses in yet unsuspected directions, but also to less obvious matters. The design of the front forks, for example: to get the curve just right, not only by gross functional criteria but also by eye, is no trivial matter. A comparison could be made with cylindrical pots of identical form on which the glaze is progressively varied, or which are very slightly modified in their proportions. Such adjustments are of the essence in realizing a design far beyond the diagram of its intended life (which can be intellectually appraised) and towards its final form; to experience such work can be deeply educative. Considerations of texture, scale, colour, tone, and the radius of an edge; the quality of a curve known so well to a boatbuilder in fairing off a sheer-strake: in getting these things right, or as right as judgement has to concede, the designer employs a concentration, and an artistry, of a different order to that which earlier stages employ – with the aid of logic and rational enquiry. Those stages always seem incredibly far distant.

The designer who does not come to feel naturally for these things (given enough self-training) is as deprived as someone who says 'I don't fancy the physical side of my love-life'. There are many aids to such self-training. No opportunity should be lost for making comparisons. For instance, students should always look at walls attentively, the plainer the better. Observe the fleeting differences of light and shade, surface, colour, and texture. Imagine one quality of surface replaced by another, and the difference it would make. See how a volume is affected by its planes and their surface qualities. Study brickwork and the effects not only of colour and texture gradations but of different types of pointing. Become aware that within the possibilities of raked pointing there are many distinctions. Confront some of the best small Georgian brick houses; see them first through half-closed eyes just as boxes with perforated holes; then gradually allow the subtlety of detailing, material, and proportion, to establish itself. In typography such matters are taken for granted. Letter forms are finely distinguished and letter-spacing of capitals is still practised, though by no means invariably. In asymmetric typography the possibilities are clearer, because logical distinctions and hierarchies of meaning can be pointed up by very small adjustments of relationship on the page. In raising consciousness of these matters, it should be remembered that our civilization sells itself through sensation, preferably with the volume turned up. This is good reason for designers to learn how to speak quietly, and to understand how it is that conversation becomes possible between people and things. There are good illustrated books to help with such studies. Examples are Gordon Cullen's *Townscape*, Elisabeth Beazley's *Design and detail of the space between buildings*, and Peter Smithson's *Bath: walks within walls*.

Returning to another false definition of design capability, it is surely foolish to suppose that everything in the world must be continuously remade or rebuilt, yet students are made to feel inadequate it they do anything less. Such pretensions must involve quite a waste of human energy and much disappointment, they also demean the possibilities we have, for learning from each other. It is becoming recognized, slowly, that buildings should be readapted to fresh uses wherever possible; the poor have always involuntarily recycled kids' toys and clothing. There are still many appliances that could do with improving, bringing up to date, or simply resuscitating. This has happened recently to some extent with wood-burning and other solid-fuel stoves; in the same area, there are many efficient paraffin devices awaiting rescue. The requirement may sometimes seem to be that of 'styling', when (say) a given mechanical principle is accepted without serious change. In a sense it is, but not in the way of imposing a style, or a concealment, upon a naked mechanism, as finding the clothes that may suit, and express, its own internal life. If this is a little too anthropomorphic, the fault is here on the right side. This is only one of many possible design activities which (like interior design) are interpretative in their nature, and which could offer a contribution within the spectrum of 'adapt, adjust, make do, mend, and develop': as distinct from 'erase, forget, and innovate'. Much can be learned from this humane preoccupation. As for colleges that stress innovation and 'originality' far too heavily, it is doubtful whether the 'look Ma no hands' content of a degree show will ever lose its appeal (to students, their relatives, and college staff), but perhaps these occasions might be put on a more kindly footing. Before leaving the subject, it might be said – and not too quietly – that the modern movement has always opposed the pettiness and irrelevance of competitive originality, and can well support the propositions in these paragraphs without historical inconsistency; though, if this were not the case, it would also be within the spirit of the modern movement to change its mind.

Two further examples must complete the account of design possibilities begun in this part. A furniture designer is considering the design of a sideboard, and let it be supposed, to simplify matters, that the design brief is very open. If you were the designer, how might you view such an opportunity? To start with you would probably have ideas of your own, but let these be put to one side (not to be lost, but returned to). You will know that the word 'sideboard' means that a certain commonly recognizable piece of furniture has emerged out of history. The origins of the piece are interesting, and perhaps suggestive, but you will question whether these old uses now exist, or exist in that form. Do the furnishing contexts of houses today, and the way people now live, suggest that 'sideboards' still do the same job? You might recall Rietveld's work on this problem, and what it had to say so presciently: 'here is a contingent equation, the elements and components of a sideboard reaching out and dissolving away into new meanings, new relationships with what surrounds them, a question implicit in an answer' (I hasten to say that this is my own response, not Rietveld's). What will be the surrounding conditions? As has been said about chair design, in practice the brief will close around the limits of the possible: marketing policy, a 'range of furniture', estimated demand, and so forth, are the governing factors in the retail market. User-context does not exist, is unknowable, except indirectly through the operation of supply and demand: furniture is really designed for the shop buyers who make sales policy. It is inevitable that design takes place on a stylistic footing, ringing the changes annually to stimulate the market. The possibilities widen in some of the more specialized or design-conscious shops, and of course dramatically so in the one-off sector – which is where it all happens for design that is formally innovative.

It should be clear that beyond the doodles in a designer's sketchbook there is no such thing as an open brief. There will always be limitations of context if not of contract; and those of cost, materials, and the special conditions of manufacture. The identification of such limits, and the turning of them to constructive account, goes hand in hand with an analysis of use, of performance. In the case of the sideboard, just what is a 'board' and a 'side'? If it is a storage cabinet, what is being stored, why, for whom, for what purposes? Are the contents used regularly – all the contents, or are some virtually dead storage? Should they be there at all? What order and kind of accessibility is implied? Why are the contents screened? – to keep out dust, or to keep out of sight and mind? Is there a temperature or humidity problem? Might there be? What is the 'top' and what is it used for? Is there necessarily a back and a front? In answering these questions and many more, it may be helpful to use a degree of abstraction as a tool of analysis – or perhaps it is better to say, as an analytical resource. For instance, for my own work I devised the categories of surface, container, support, threshold, screen, connector, traverse, grip, and mechanism. By such analytical procedures it is possible to dismantle an object which may have lost its reasons for existence, and to reconstruct it in new terms. The object as such may disappear if its meaning is better seen in some more, selective or more comprehensive arrangement of parts – 'parts' being here, the purposes served. Thus, for instance, wardrobes disappear into storage walls – conceptually, but not on the retail market, which remains object-fixated although tending to respond to appearances.

For designers the real difficulties do not occur at an analytical level – the determining of relationships – but in the realization of a design, against criteria that become increasingly elusive. This is the realm of the senses, of imagination, and of judgement. The design *may* exhibit an intellectual proposition, or an argument that can be 'read' and for which the key premises may be available to inference. This is unlikely to be more than one dimension of meaning in the job and rarely an essential one – except to the designer, whose satisfaction it may be to write in to the job a clear level of argument as an optional reading, free of any impairment to its more ordinary usefulness. In his analytical work the designer seeks a sense of priority in the work and a full understanding of the conditions that must determine its life. He may seek also a 'diagram of correspondence' to help him – not to dodge his constraints, to get round them, but to take them up, to identify their potential, and to use this potential to positive advantage. As has been said earlier, this conversion of constraint into opportunity is about as good a definition of design as any. The sideboard may well disappear as a recognizable entity and its functions disappear into new relationships. It should be noted, however, how many presuppositions of economic openness have been necessary even to make this discussion possible.

For social and economic reasons design is far from being an open-ended activity; yet, it is an insistent requirement of modern design that openness and intelligibility should characterize its products; that life should be free to flow through them, that their meaning should be defined – indeed, made accessible, by projections of reference that are strictly outside the problem itself. Designers in some fields will have seen an object developing into a system, system into process, and process into information, in a way that disconcertingly suggests that their world is dissolving away around them. In making finite decisions they will be aware of a new dimension of reference in their thinking. This is the simplest consequence of a changing world picture, expressed in the physical sciences, philosophy, the arts, communications technology, and elsewhere. A highly particularized design solution – say a one-off job with clear determinants from place and occasion – must now not only exhibit a field of generic reference, but derive a gain in particularity from it. Once this design requirement is identified, felt for (it does not have to be an intellectual quest), it will become clear that the survival of modern design, and its character, is inseparable from the interdependence of modern man, the principles of mutuality that knit together his societies, and the altered view he now has of his world, as distinct from that of his village. He does indeed occupy perhaps more consciously a village, but with an altered frame of reference.

Such perceptions have their equivalent in design education. The textile designer who has never felt for the distinctions of outlook implied by (say) Ronchamp, the Barcelona Pavilion, and the Dymaxion house (a specially indigestible mix), or has never distinguished between the geometry of a cube and an inflated structure, is simply working as a badly educated specialist. If on the other hand, such understanding is achieved, there is no loss of focus or immediacy in the designer's own work, but it may well be helped to refer outwards and gain some reinforcement of meaning thereby. The designer's intuitions will be instructed by a richer sense of the place he occupies. There is a parallel with analytical procedure. In forming a hypothesis, the designer will not only have a picture of prior demand to test it against – this is professional necessity – but he will also find that when a hypothesis suddenly springs into consciousness, it is instructed, fitting the conditions of the job rather than arbitrary conditions – and this is creative necessity. When something goes wrong, it can usually be traced back to the beginning, from the acceptance of false premises. Hence on the one hand the importance of questions, and on the other, of the resourcefulness of attitude that prompts them. Such basic requirements (asking the right questions, knowing how to, and mustering the will) are far from being naturally coterminous. This is why technique must be kind to the user and not only 'technically effective'. To use a designer's figure of speech, if the cross-sectional area of personality fails to be exposed to the creative possibilities in a job, so that when necessary the designer can get his weight behind his imagination, then the situation can easily become a sterile one. Technique has a core structure that is irreducible, and possessed by an elementary logic and sequence, but it can be used, and interpreted, with a great deal of personal latitude.

The last example of design opportunities is well discussed by Papanek and others (so it will be only touched upon briefly here), namely, that of inventive design in so many obvious areas of social and personal deprivation, where the look of something and the pleasure of handling or contemplating its qualities are still very relevant, but may have to be strictly secondary to producing it cheaply, getting it marketed, and ensuring that it works for its living. Equipment for the handicapped is a case in point. This work is often close to the engineering end of the design spectrum. Advocates of such work sometimes seem to twist the arm of students into thinking that only preoccupations of this kind are socially responsible. This is a false view, though not unsympathetic. It might be said that two design jobs in the first half of this century have been brilliantly apt, inventive, and economical. One is the design of the cat's-eye for road transport and the other is the design of the London Underground map. In fact the cat's-eye considered merely as an item of manufacture, is a very nice piece of anonymous sculpture, and its self-cleaning rubber eye-lid is a concept masterly in its essential simplicity – but nobody digs up cat's-eyes to admire their form, the important thing is that they work so extraordinarily well. The one job is superbly inventive, the other a first-class ordering of information – a model of its kind. However, it is a mistake to suppose that designers can freely elect to design the equivalents for cat's-eyes, and London Underground maps, or mechanical equipment for handicapped children. The same goes for the trailing link baby-buggy, which must have eased life's burden for so many harassed mothers getting on and off buses with children, or out shopping. An aptitude for mechanical invention is one kind of design skill and it is also a personal design aptitude; not all designers can work in this way, or are naturally drawn to it, whatever view they may take of the moral imperatives that seem to beckon their commitment. Designers must find out just where, within the very wide design spectrum, their own individual contribution can be most effective.

Several conclusions may be drawn – tentatively – from this discussion. The first is that design opportunities are so various and plentiful, and designers so different in their natural capability, that it is rash to generalize too far about the way in which they do (or should) approach their work. Second, it is clear that analytical thinking may profit from insights that are interdisciplinary; practical design procedures are necessarily so. This is certainly the case up to that familiar and pleasing stage in design work, when the categories of requirement in a job suddenly seem to be matching nicely with the categories of a possible answer. The third conclusion is that this kind of thinking, together with simple problem-solving procedure, is quite natural to design work, but not rigidly or predictably so, over the middle range of the design spectrum (see part 1) – and hardly at all in certain areas. The productive relevance of any design procedure is partly a function of the designer's personality; procedures only exist for people who employ them. Other things being equal, those most acceptable will be closest to the exercise of judgement in ordinary life. If this is so, then it may well be that the ordinary syntactic 'thinking-out-loud' and relatively loose-fit and two-way devices like the report (see part 16) have been somewhat underestimated in favour of logical models of greater sophistication, even though such models have had to be partly dismantled to accommodate objections. In short, it is probably useful to recognize a distinction between technique and method, taking the latter no further than the more lenient notion of 'procedure'.

The natural limitation of such a view is the range of work with which this book is properly concerned. Within this range it is always tempting to confuse logical modes of thinking with the untidy and informal procedures that usually prompt fruitful ideas into being. As is commonly known, the best ideas often occur at odd moments on the backs of old envelopes. Computer-aided analytical technique becomes necessary as the scale of the work increases – and moves off the stage of this book – and as the conditions for its measurable efficiency become both critical and manifold. Where very complex constraints are concerned, as in planning the co-ordination of operations on a large building site, the job cannot be fumbled as far as an analysis of quantities is concerned. For any work with expressive latitude, it is still necessary to define its extent. But in the work discussed here, analytical thinking has the secondary (but crucial) function of presenting the designer to the work in a responsive frame of mind, and in good heart. For some people, reliance on sequential method will paralyse rather than quicken their responses.

The worst error is to take refuge in notions of 'method' or 'process' at the cost of any practical commitment. Thus is a wilderness created by default, and argued for in retrospect by a specious appeal to scientific method in the way the problem was approached. Sir Peter Medawar reminded us that the scientific hypothesis takes the form of a hunch, or an intelligent guess, which is then scrupulously examined against existing schemata to see if it works. Not that such comparisons throw a direct light upon the designer's role, which is to be available to tasks for which his experience is fitting, in full awareness that some things are much better done by people for themselves.

A socially adaptive view of design practice takes the view that a designer accepts what he is given, and makes the best of it, by knowing how to weigh up his constraints shrewdly and logically. This is a perilously inadequate view of adaptation, as can be seen in every area of society where new adaptations to reality are breaking through old and outworn assumptions. Designers must themselves adapt to a changing picture of their professional role and its validity. As was argued on different grounds in part 4, the modern movement advances by fruitful hypothesis, which is often code-breaking. It steps sideways, by an elegant or 'fitting' alternative; and it steps backward by keeping up appearances. Fortunately, falling into disrepute a little, its adherents can relax and accept their common human failings.

Choosing, therefore, a more homely language: a designer must have his tools around him in the ordinary way of competence. A good joiner, who knows (as the saying is) seasoned wood from green, will have in his toolkit a few tools that are rarely used but irreplaceable when needed; he must know how to use them and when to pick them up. A designer's priority is openness of creative response, the capacity to mix the levels of his thinking, to ask productive questions; he must seek the personal conditions that help him to work in that way, and the social conditions that allow him to. This search will not prevent him getting on with the job at the limits of the possible, keeping all his tools sharp for the next chance to make himself useful.

The artist

The artist: disciple, abundant, multiple, restless.
The true artist: capable, practising, skilful;
maintains dialogue with his heart, meets things with his mind.

The true artist: draws out all from his heart,
works with delight, makes things with calm, with sagacity,
works like a true Toltec, composes his objects, works dextrously,
arranges materials, adorns them, makes them adjust, invents.

The carrion artist: works at random, sneers at the people,
makes things opaque, brushes across the surface of the face of things,
works without care, defrauds people, is a thief.

Toltec poem translated from the Spanish by Denise Levertov

6 Designer as artisan

It is well known that many designers have their own small work-shop, for modelmaking, for making up and testing full-size details, for prototype work, and sometimes simply for play – which is not only a relief from the drawing board, but can prove directly and unexpectedly helpful to any job on hand. Industrial product design-ers will usually have access to factory facilities for prototype work, or may co-operate with the research and development group already attached to the factory. In Scandinavia, it is not uncommon to find designers operating their own studio/workshops in direct associa-tion with a manufacturer – a large proportion of their time being given to the production needs of the factory, but some to their own more personal work, which may, or may not, ultimately serve the interests of their hosts. This degree of subsidized independence is a shrewdly practical arrangement on both sides, because the manu-facturer will pick up any benefit from a designer whose work is going well; but it does imply a restricted field, and ties that a de-signer may not always find acceptable. It works best for specialists (in glass, pottery, furniture, for example). Obviously a product de-signer will always need close contact with a client's technical staff, if he is working to a tight brief and to all the limiting conditions of a particular production set-up and its marketing potential. In these circumstances the private workshop will be less useful – or even misleading. However, it is a modest technical base within which to experiment and improvise.

The artisan designer is a different animal altogether, often equally remote from the drawing board and from the corridors of management; engaging directly in the business of small-scale production which may necessarily include marketing and distribu-tion. The artisan is a blue-collar worker, he wears overalls (or needs to), has dust in his hair, and gets his hands dirty. Inescapably, he partakes of behaviour patterns that distinguish working men from higher management, though he will earn rather less, work longer hours, and will approach his work with aims and standards that tradesmen will not normally articulate, or even find sympathetic. Thus among fellow workers the artisan will feel somewhat estranged, though sharing, at some levels, much of their culture; with business men and white-collar designers (particularly architects) he may feel equally uncomfortable, though for different reasons. For academic and design theorists he will feel the least sympathy – although artisans often teach – probably because they seem to him to speak from a distasteful blend of economic privilege and practical ignorance. Well-off left-wingers are unpopular for similar reasons. The artisan identifies strongly with the 'shop floor'; anyone who pontificates without having done their time at the bench, or minding a machine, is felt to be automatically disqualified, and not to be taken seriously.

Thus it will be seen that the working stance of an artisan can become at once isolated and prone to internal contradictions, for reasons that are inherently class-related. Add to this his continuously insecure economic footing, and the contradictions implicit in his marketing problems (at worst, he may be producing peasant-revival knick-knacks for middle-class weekenders), and it is then possible to see how so many small workshops are cut off from the intellectual currents of their time, and produce work that is self-contained, sentimental, and backward-looking. However, in the late 1960s and in the 1970s there was a revival of enthusiasm for this way of working. This followed naturally and properly enough from the energy crisis (or rather, the abrupt public awakening to its existence), a renewed interest in conservation and the need for a decentralized economy, and from the growth of attitudes celebrated, typically, in E. F. Schumacher's *Small is beautiful*, and in the writings of Ivan Illich. That all this was placed in a forward-looking context by Kropotkin (*Fields, factories and workshops*) writing in 1898, is neither here nor there. More interesting for present purposes is the coming-full-circle of the modern movement, and what seems to be the historical moment for a reappraisal of this way of working. Anyone who doubts the valid scale of small workshops (assuming they survive at all) should not only contemplate the minuscule attainment of modern design through factory production over the past fifty years, but should read Percy Mitchell's *A boatbuilder's story* – a real eye-opener as to what can be done by a few men working with primitive equipment and against unbelievable practical hardships. These are the extremes: at a less strenuous level, and given that an artisan's life is problematical, over-worked, and under-paid, what reasons might there be for a designer choosing it?

Elective affinity is the most understandable reason – a liking for tools and materials and for the grounded nature of this way of working; with its converse, a disinclination to work so remotely from the final product, a dislike of paper work, and a mistrust of offices and all that they can seem to imply of the clerkly life. Against the attractions of workshops, which are only too easy to romanticize, must be set the severe limitations of scale that any workshop must accept (and which some designers find frustrating), the long hours, and all the anxieties and privations that attend self-employment at a relatively low standard of living. Such constraints will prove a stimulus to some people and a discouragement to others. The skills required are – surprisingly – not much of a problem. Trade practice is always hedged about with thorny growths of technical mystification, so that 'their' patch is not too easily trodden over or under-valued. In college technical shops, the women starting from scratch are always surprised by how quickly they come to feel at home. This is not to say that standards are easy to establish and maintain, or that craft skills demand much less than a working lifetime for their full mastery; but an intelligent and willing person who really concentrates, can learn the elements of workshop practice in far less time than is taken for a full trade apprenticeship (granted, admittedly, some initial aptitude, which it is fair to presuppose).

Some designers are driven to experiment with workshops, often quite late in their working life, in an emotional response to the logic of their own perceptions. They may feel that in western societies, the only people who can afford design services are those who already have more than they need, and that therefore, 'professional' designing is a form of cake decoration when the rest of the world needs bread. Alternatively, and relatedly, they may decide that managerial posturing is no way forward in the frequent confrontations between workers and management, and that the decent thing is to withdraw from the prior status-assurance (and salary structure) that the professions are in being to ensure for their members. It must be said at once that artisans have no way of opting out of their society –

except into the illusion of total self-sufficiency, that final parody of the mutual aid principle – because the alternative networks of distribution and exchange do not in fact exist (or not as yet) except in small and occasional areas of social experimentation. Workshops depend like everybody else on an open-market economy.

However, there are certain existential advantages in the workshop situation. First, a service workshop (see below) can integrate itself into a local community in a very direct way. Such a workshop grows and proceeds through personal encounters; which keeps every option open and, in a sense, renewed. The opportunities for experimental design work will be, proportionately, few; but their context will be organically provided for in a possible widening of acceptance as the workshop gradually builds up local confidence in its services. Second, in any kind of workshop there is a natural give and take that acts as a control, giving immediacy and proportion to its activities; and there is continuous feedback both in the way of working, and probably through the marketing arrangements. Third, in the cultural desert that we would all like to fertilize with new vernacular life, it may be more satisfactory to make things (and to make them well) than to talk about it, or to issue instructions.

Broadly speaking there are two ways of working as an artisan: with a service workshop, or in production. In the former case the workshop serves local needs and is open to whatever comes through the door on Monday mornings – just as a garage is. The service workshop emphasizes the one-off product (in the case of a joinery shop this might be anything from a staircase to a shop-fitting job or an exhibition stand) and occasionally the service as such (e.g. repairs and renewals); there may also be a production bread-and-butter line to help keep things going. The production shop is far more common and of course for many years studio potters have worked in this way, which (by simple definition) implies that the designer has a range of products in mind to begin with, or that possibility as an aim, and then sets up a workshop to make them. Other things being equal, it is very desirable that the production workshop has its own retail shop. Transport costs are reduced (the customers do the travelling), middle-men's (legitimate) profits are eliminated, packing and storage problems are minimized, other people's products can be sold, and that mysterious entity 'goodwill' is fostered, because your customers come back to you (products sold on the open market simply disappear). Shops are common as boutiques, or attached to potteries, but less common elsewhere (perhaps because other things rarely *are* equal).

It seems to be the general experience that there is no lack of work for artisans in any field: the problem lies in sustaining the first two years. It is decidedly a mistake for design theorists to suppose that every serious design opportunity must refer back either to the type-form (a myth with Platonic overtones) or to the special conditions of mass production, when in fact other demands are real enough and can often accommodate a more flexible response, both as to design and to the means of production. Not only is 'custom' work (one-offs) an economic proposition, but very often short production runs are better handled by small producers. Such work will include jobbing printing, exhibition and shopfitting work, purpose-made furniture for hostels, schools, laboratories, hotels, etc, interior conversion work, package furniture, and other possibilities too numerous to mention. Production facilities will normally include as much mechanization as the shop can reasonably afford, but the machines will be of the open-ended type that extend the hand rather than replace it. (For example: a joinery shop of this sort would have a router, spindle, dovetailer, mortiser, in addition to the usual saw-bench and planers, etc; but would be unlikely to have a multiple jig borer, variable offset lathes, or a four-cutter.) It is a serious mistake to begin with portable electric handtools on the supposition that these machines will fulfil anything like their theoretical capabilities (and be otherwise attractive for their sheer portability): far better to spend the money on heavy second-hand equipment. This is almost a general law for all trades, and all knowledgeable tradesmen confirm it. Heavy castings soak up vibration and are safer and far less tiring to use: where cutters are involved, they will tend to hold their edge better where chatter is eliminated. However, such matters belong to the delights of homespun technical controversy and are outside the scope of this book.

What are the worst difficulties? The most serious is the need for adequate working capital. Long term loans, and accompanying advice, may be available from government-supported bodies. Without some years of practical experience (meaning, doing it the hard way) it is common to take rather too rosy a view of the financial difficulties. Beginners overlook the need for reserves against slow payment (some reputable big stores take 3 to 6 months to pay), against bad debts (clients who may not pay at all) and the costs of advertising, transport, cleaning, postage, travel, etc, apart from the more obvious overheads like rent, heating, light, and power, the need to allow for holidays and sick time, the cost of time spent chatting to people and doing the book-keeping, and the many other matters that may tip the balance between ruin and success. Form-fillers and officials of all kinds are the nightmare anxieties of any artisan's life – as indeed of any self-employed person – and records tend to become scanty, episodic, or lost in brown paper bags under benches.

The problem of locale may be set up, or solved, by personal considerations, or by happy accident; otherwise, and given an entirely open situation, it is more difficult. Workshops must keep in touch with their market, and enough customers, yet city premises have high overheads; a cheaper place in the country may either involve high transport costs, or may force the decision to service local demand. Beginners usually underestimate floor space. The problem here is keeping various operations and storage provisions sufficiently distinct, or actually sealed from each other in the case of dusty operations like wood machining. In a joinery shop for instance, assembly must be separated from machining and separate space may be needed both as a dust-free polishing and/or spray shop and perhaps for packing and storage. The latter will comprise both finished work and component parts. All this will naturally follow from the nature of the shop and its products, but this may not be easily predictable at the time that premises are secured. It is therefore wise to allow generously at the outset or to try to find premises with some expansion possibility. In the cities, co-operatives are possible; and of course workshops can be run in this way – indeed there is no limit to the variety of options available. Some of the craftier workshops – those that look back to the Gimson and Barnsley tradition of fine one-off pieces – have developed to its logical extreme the possible expensiveness of hand-built work (a deeply unattractive option but showing the range of the spectrum). Such a heavily stressed craft approach is no doubt a good survival strategy in its own terms. Some artisans can get a little part-time teaching to help out. Often this doesn't work, the two worlds being so far apart; but sometimes it does.

Another difficulty is that of work coming in at the wrong time. Turning down work makes for bad relations, delivering it very late is considerably worse, and rushing the job at cost to technical standards is worst of all. Under these circumstances, it is hard to find a balance between a properly equipped and economically viable small workshop, and its necessary escalation into small-scale factory production, with all the economic and personal pressures that this may imply. Some factories have begun in just this way – Terence Conran's was an example – and have continued to maintain conscientious design standards, if at some cost to the original intentions of the designer; but at some point an artisan must decide in principle how much he wants to expand (if the possibility presents itself) and how such expansion might affect the personal goals he has set himself.

Having reviewed the possibilities, and the hazards attached to them, it remains to point out that very few workshops are informed by the kind of design consciousness that designers (as met with in this book) might promptly recognize. And looking at workshops from the designer's point of view, some designers will find it relevant to try the artisan's approach during some part of their working lives – perhaps for some of the reasons already suggested, but also because the problems in design that most interest them are best pursued by these means (which include, of course, the benefit of well-understood production constraints). Different again is the situation of designers who are able to use some of the resources to be found in college workshops; though here not only is the situation academically subsidized, but in the nature of things, direct production can only be occasional. There is of course the academic tradition of the limited edition, often of parochial interest to the college concerned, but when work of a wider appeal emerges from the presses its graphic design is rarely distinctive. The college prospectus is sometimes better conceived than its art printing.

This is the 'workshop situation' at its most attenuated and, quite characteristically, at its closest both to academic life and to the possibility of subsidy, neither of which typify its ordinary economic independence. It is the day-to-day survival problem that gives the small production unit a certain realism of outlook, and helps to offset, perhaps, too much preciousness in its design approach. It will certainly be urged, however, that even at their most robust, the small workshops make too personalized a contribution to be of much general interest, and that their production potential is so small, that designers will hardly wish to take them seriously. To this charge, an artisan might reply 'never mind the width, mate, feel the quality' and then, looking more closely, he might add: 'where is this width anyway; what can you show for your vastly superior resources?' At a deeper level of argument, the notional value of direct production is defensible on rather different grounds, with less emphasis on the product. With his usual clear-sightedness, W. R. Lethaby made short work of the task. The occasion was a public presentation at the Central School in honour of his sixty-fifth birthday (1922). 'What I seem to have found out about life' he gave as follows.

1   Life is best thought of as service.
2   Service is first of all, and of greatest necessity, common productive work.
3   The best way to think of labour is as art ... By welcoming it, and thinking of it as art, the slavery of labour may be turned into joy.
4   Art is best thought of as fine and sound ordinary work. So understood, it is the widest, best and most necessary form of culture.
5   Culture should be thought of as not only book-learning, but as a tempered human spirit. A shepherd, ship-skipper or carpenter enjoys a different culture from the book-scholar, but it is nonetheless a true culture.

When a man of Lethaby's substance adds up the lessons of his life, it behoves lesser men to be quiet a minute. Could it be that here is a responsibility that the workshops assume, and that the rest of us might indeed take more seriously. For such a redefinition of culture, the artisan approach is in principle a model contribution, in an area of conflict providing one of the deepest problems of reconciliation that confronts our epoch.

During the 1970s the Construction School in the West of England College of Art, Bristol, began to address its energies to the future of the artisan designer. Several workshops resulted, directly or indirectly. The development of an educational approach at degree level (only educationalists understand what this means) is by no means easy, because, as has been indicated, nothing is further from the hard truths of a workshop situation than the free-and-easy ambience of a college studio. The immediate difficulties are: those of extended reference (what this book is about) to counter the particularity of the various production disciplines (whether of hand or machine); the gaining of technical understanding at the right level of complexity; finding the right teachers, particularly those with a broad enough design commitment; and stepping round the worst craft whimsicalities that seem to beset this scale of work. The development of a suitable framework for studies is a long-term project, subject to a good deal of trial and error. It is unfortunate that in the case of Bristol, its development was cut short by the CNAA closing the Construction School, thus losing, in this context at least, the contributions from experienced tutors in the field. (The history of this School is outlined in part 22.)

If unfortunate, then perhaps – other things being equal – to be expected. In Britain, for example, degree-receiving (and awarding) is essentially the dream and the prerogative of the would-be grammar school boy or girl, not to mention their sometimes pushy parents. For this very reason degrees are taken so seriously just a little further down the social gradient. Ceramics and textiles have always had a strong middle-class following, but otherwise the chap who is 'good with his hands' may be felt to belong down the corridor with the trade apprentices, who are always something of an embarrassment to the higher educationalists. ('Good with his hands' – the phrase needs turning over in the mind to receive its full measure.) However, a design-conscious artisan will certainly be uncomfortable with the apprentices; so, except in the very few senior 'vocational' courses, which because of their reduced status carry a penalty for those who teach in them, the design artisan may feel as ill-at-ease in the colleges as in society at large.

As to the transition from college to workshop, Michael Rowbottom (teaching at Bristol) advanced the practical suggestion that students might learn a general theory of machines (and much else) by designing and building their own. Once the materials have been paid for, the machines could then be used in their own workshops, thus easing the awkward problem of starting-capital for beginners. The same could be done for benching, racking, and all the jigs and appliances that a workshop needs. Not all educational establishments would support such notions, and the experimental work to beef them up. Training colleges are often the most prone to doing things 'by the book' but alas they are not alone in this failing. A cynic might suggest that such ideas are too obviously useful and forward-looking to interest educationalists. Ivan Illich might add – well, what do you expect; and a harassed administrator might retort that the principles of public accountability cannot embrace the support of free enterprise. Be that as it may, there is now a demand from young people for an artisan-type education, as distinct from a technical training, and viewed as a special case of design education of the normal kind. No doubt a widening of response will become apparent.

Artisans of all ages have no problem in finding plenty to read, especially in the technical literature. The 'giant home workshop manuals' are often strewn with useful advice. From a designer's point of view, much of it succumbs to the false status and the craft-conscious eclecticism that disfigures so many workshop projects; but, with this reservation, the USA has been a good source for practical manuals of all kinds. With historical references of such high calibre as Salaman's *Dictionary of tools* no one will despair of their bedside reading for quite a long time to come. Three books of wider interest might be mentioned: George Sturt's well-known and evocative *The wheelwright's shop*, Ashbee's *Craftsmanship in competitive industry* – a fascinating historical document invoking Ashbee's very characteristic notion of 'standard' – and the more recent *The nature and art of workmanship* by David Pye.

In summary, it may be said that the workshop way of life is hard work, immensely educative, often enjoyable, and usually underpaid; it stands on its own feet better than some of the alternatives. It is doubtful if what we may call 'design workshops' will ever organize themselves into presenting a coherent viewpoint, or a representative body of work. There is never much time to spare, even for taking photographs. Nor do such self-observations feel quite appropriate. Perhaps this is the one case where a failure to stand up and be counted is almost enviably reticent. However, good workshops – no doubt rare – are worth seeking out, and occasionally they might offer a useful design apprenticeship.

7   Reading for design

Designers who earn a living by design, seldom have the time to read many design books. Except – as theatre people understand so well – when resting. Trade catalogues and the journals can be quite enough. Thus the main burden falls upon critics and design theorists, who read each other's books most assiduously. College students and their teachers struggle to keep up, putting in, probably, the most tenacious mileage overall; whilst the public at large, users of the things that designers produce, are understandably less concerned to read about them. It may be true that book-learning never made a designer; indeed, the best informed and most articulate people may be the least directly productive. This is no reason for students to cherish a defensive ignorance of their subject. The notion that designers should be noble savages living-it-down in teepee settlements, is not unreservedly appealing, but even this can be consulted in the literature. As for intending teachers, it would be nice if they could distinguish between William, Henry, and Charles Morris, and perhaps know that Black Mountain was a college (and a good one). Actually there are enough books and magazines to please most people. Given the will, an open mind, and a good pair of eyes, what is the best way to set about an investigation?

The following notes develop a simple-minded strategy, in the form of map-making. By this means, an apprehensive student can hold the whole situation in the palm of his hand, and decide how best to serve his own priorities. The authors and titles mentioned are specimen attractions to be met with in any given area. The selection has no claim to infallibility, in the way of offering the 'best' or the latest books – which tend to be around in the studios anyway – but has two purposes: to body forth some of the ideas that appear in this book, and to draw attention to some of the older sources that might otherwise be overlooked. Like buildings, books should be left to settle for a few years before being taken too seriously. It is fair to claim that all recommendations are worth, at least, a close look; but the argument does not depend upon their acceptance. If some books are out of print, this is not unusual. Design students soon learn that almost everything worth having is nearly unobtainable ('sorry Sir, there was never any demand'). Books are no exception, but all books are available to those who want them enough. Librarians are usually very helpful. (Part 17 gives bibliographical details of the titles mentioned here.)

What sort of books is it useful for a designer to read? The answer has to be, that with respect to designing, any sort that helps the job along: that musters energy in the first place, and that then helps to direct such energy where and how it is needed. Obviously this is a personal matter. It may be equally obvious that a designer will ask of his reading a deepened understanding of his own craft, and of the cultural matrix of its forming – complex and almost unending as such studies can prove to be. However, such reading will certainly include books with no ostensible bearing upon the contingencies of design practice. Such books may (for instance) nourish or encourage creative attitudes (or states of mind, of feeling, sensation, intuition) that are helpfully propulsive to creative activity in a general way, and to a design commitment in particular; just as the experience of music or poetry or mathematics might do – not merely with potency, but with resonance. This might be true for the sense in which Ernest Newman described an effect of Beethoven's music: 'It is the peculiarity of Beethoven's imagination that again and again he lifts us to a height from which we revaluate not only all music but all life, all emotion, and all thought.' Such considerations throw into relief the philistinism of training courses (and less) that masquerade as an education, and whose idea of a 'booklist' may be somewhat cut-and-dried. However, in their support it must be said that C. R. Ashbee had his apprentices doing physical jerks (pictured in *Craftsmanship in competitive industry*) and perhaps he found that this was just as good. The following notes take a fairly broad view of what it might be useful to read, and their logic must be left to unfold toward the recommendations that end the part.

The map proposed has twenty-seven areas, or categories, serving to distinguish (functionally) one kind of book from another. Books that elude any such classification can then be considered separately (or quietly escape attention). The special advantage of what seems, at first sight, a rather unattractive exercise in category-for-mation, is that component books can be added to, or subtracted from, any one category, if the reader wishes eventually to keep abreast of his subject. Thus the inevitable 'dating' of any one contribution in no way impairs the strength of the group – considered as evidence – which, in turn, enables a first-class book that may be getting a bit long in the tooth still to have the sympathetic attention that it deserves. It is easy to become a little patronizing as such a book slips back into history. A good example is Herbert Read's *Art and industry*. This book is useful in a minor way – to compare Bayer's typography and layout (first edition) with the tweedy British aftermath. However, it is also still the best available account of its subject, and generally speaking, it is also the best illustrated. However, the book was first published in 1934. If Read were alive today he would no doubt tighten up the argument in a few places (in others, relax it), and he would certainly wish to reselect a few illustrations of product design. A final – and related – advantage of the territorial decentralization proposed, is that nobody's toes are trodden on. If the functional distinctions are reasonably argued, and useful, then students can confidently find their way around to the point where such aids are superfluous.

One question will certainly be asked (it always is). Why so many architects in a book about design? If the profession is only half as bad as its critics insist – as pompous, as falsely omniscient, and as socially divisive – should we have any truck with them at all? Malcolm MacEwan remarks how well the RIBA building in London expresses all this, and how lastingly. Time has added a dimension of irony to this building's monumental self-regard. Does this mean that in the end, all architecture, like poetry, *must* tell the truth, however hard it tries, so we all get the buildings we deserve?

These are difficult matters. The architects mentioned here are hardly a fair sample of the profession at large (and it is very large), and those who write about architecture are hardly more so. However, as A. N. Whitehead said, 'you may not divide the seamless coat of learning', and this is true for the whole development of modern design. It so happens, for reasons that are by no means inscrutable (but which it would be tedious to examine here) that architects have articulated the critical attitudes that belong to that development. Furthermore, in their one-off buildings there was far more scope for experimentation, and for the manipulation of space and form, than has been available in product design. As is well known, however, most of the significant furniture design of this century has come from designers with an architectural training (this is the way the word 'architect' is used throughout this book) so a distinction is unreal at that level.

It is obvious enough that building design provides an accommodating umbrella to shelter many of the smaller-scaled and more intimate design opportunities. From a co-operative standpoint, the question is one of attitude rather than scale (that 'consciousness in common' of which Michael Kullman speaks), unless it is felt that at all costs designers should be prevented from combining (it goes to their heads). For the present, design students risk an impoverishment of their work if they attempt to study one design category in conceptual isolation from its neighbours (and parents). At a practical level, the way architects understand manufacture, and close-range detailing, is often stereotyped or painfully vague and abstract; such that architectural students could well profit from a closer experience of the workshops found in design schools. Similarly, while the more pedestrian design schools are crassly ignorant of modern architecture, it is also not uncommon to meet architectural tutors who have not even heard of the Bill–Tschichold controversy; far from being aware of its special interest. However, such reservations do nothing to weaken the obvious case for articulating a common critical tradition wherever voices can be found to speak up from first-hand experience; adding such testimony to the work of the professional critics. The life and work of Walter Gropius, what designer's work has not, indirectly, been touched by this man? The remarkable thing is not the commonly accessible nature of one designer's work to another, but that false barriers have persisted so long – and particularly in design education.

1   It remains to add that the worst design books are not usually the work of architects. The 'coffee-table' book is little more than an extended colour-supplement. Such books – large, thick, squarish, and trendy, printed a soupy offset, plastic-covered, and lavish with art photography – such books are a menace to design students. Their imagery reveals nothing that it would be useful to know (like

the context, or the cost, or the performance, of the objects they illustrate). Students who rely heavily on this sort of book and the magazines as the full extent of their reading, will hardly be reading these lines, so this category (outside the ranks of the chosen) can be left to speak for itself, which it will do very plausibly. Such books leave the impression of nothingness; that nothing has occurred; but at first acquaintance, a lot seems to be going on.

2   Coffee-table books have their up-market relatives. Like a railway bookstall novelette compared with something by Ivy Compton Burnett, the one is easy and the other definitely sophisticated, but each may be a form of chat. Both categories profit from a willingness to sip, rather than drink deeply of their subject-matter; and their contents are often as out of key as these mixed metaphors. A good example is *Meaning in architecture* (Jencks and Baird) in which some of the brightest English-language theoreticians (Baird / Broadbent / Frampton / Jencks / Silver) all have a go, and in which the opening theme is 'semiology'. *High-tech* (by Kron and Slesin) is a rather different specimen. Apart from a certain exclusiveness in their tone of voice, such books may enliven the company of their stuffier brethren, and are even a passable substitute for conversation (in remote places).

3   The synoptic books. These informative and inspirational volumes bring together what is otherwise apart, by placing designed artefacts against parallel work in other fields (the arts, sciences, philosophy, etc.) and in the full context of their origin (for example, a context of ideas, technology, social circumstance). The extent to which historical determination is a viable tool of analysis has come under question. Books of this type sound large and difficult for beginners, and invariably are; but they are indispensable in providing frames of reference, from (or within) which, students can find a personal orientation and a sense of their own inheritance. The most influential writers of this kind (such as Lewis Mumford and Sigfried Giedion) are also, as it happens, the widest in scope. Giedion's *Space, time and architecture* and its sequel *Mechanization takes command* (to which can be added the later *Eternal present* trilogy) are excellent basic books with which to start a design library. As

is proper to their intention, they are marvellously well illustrated (Mumford relies more on his text). Giedion's work wears well (or, as a boatman might say, sits well in the water) although in recent years attended by the corrective nibblings of lesser fry; but he remains, by and large, magisterially invulnerable within the scope of his large and splendid volumes. Students might note that *Mechanization* has the only decent account (to 1989) of modern furniture, now that Gordon Logie's short book, *Furniture from machines*, is becoming hard to find.

4   The histories. These are shorter, less speculative, more specialized, than the synoptic works mentioned above. A justly well-known example is Pevsner's *Pioneers of modern design*. More a collation than a historical study is Herbert Spencer's *Pioneers of modern typography*. Certain biographical studies become historical documents in virtue of subject and authorship, and these (because of their informality) are worth watching for. William Curtis's *Modern architecture* joins Ken Frampton's similarly titled book, as recent work of substance.

5   Books on a theme (historical or otherwise): narrowing the focus. A typical historical document is the facsimile reprint of *Circle* (edited by Gabo, Martin, and Nicholson), a book that might have been written last week (but for its optimism) but was in fact published in 1937, to celebrate the return of a prodigal son (the modern movement) to these shores. Nominally concerned to emphasize 'one common idea and one common spirit: the constructive trend in the art of our day', these writings seem (implicitly) full of promises: the extent to which they were kept, is better estimated from a later survey, *The rationalists*, edited by Dennis Sharp (1978). Very different is Konrad Wachsmann's *Turning point of building*, a classic statement of the 'only connect' theme at the level of sophisticated hardware (the legendary Alexander Graham Bell steals the show, peering forth from 'a simple wooden shelter in the form of a perfect tetrahedron'). Bruce Martin, our man in junction and modular matters, has *Joints in buildings* and his interesting *Standards and building* as a British contribution.

6   Books about individual designers – Wachsmann (see 5) is al-most that – and collections of their work. Examples: the *Life* of El Lissitzky by his widow (*formidable*, as the French might say), *Wells Coates*, by S. Cantacuzino (a book generous of reference), and the many-volumed *Oeuvre complète* of Le Corbusier (the best vehicle for the study of this great master short of getting on the road). There is much to be said for in-depth studies of individual designers if the evidence is plentifully available, though, if at all feasible, their work must always be seen and touched as well as read about in books. The danger of 'contamination' by 'influences' can be left to the fantasy life of our smaller-minded pundits. It is useful to correlate observa-tion and reading with critical studies, and 7.

7   Books by designers. At best, there is a spirit and an authenticity in such writing, of an order very different from the efforts of the journalists who follow along after, doing their best to cut the Mas-ters down to size. This is certainly true of Gropius (e.g. *The new architecture and the Bauhaus*), Le Corbusier (e.g. *Towards a new ar-chitecture*) and Moholy-Nagy (e.g. *The new vision*). The same is pos-sibly true of Marx and decidedly true of Freud. Original papers are now available in collections by historians. An excellent example is Tim and Charlotte Benton's *Form and function*. Here students will find Marcel Breuer's short and very clear exposition of modern movement attitudes, 'Where do we stand?'; a voice from within.

8   Presentation and memorial volumes. Rather a special form of book compiled in honour of some retiring luminary, or perhaps after his or her death. Usually essays contributed by colleagues on any theme of mutual concern, or personal reminiscences; or both. Often such occasions draw forth informal contributions of much historical interest, of a kind that might otherwise be passed over. An outstanding example is *Planning and architecture*, essays presented to Arthur Korn (a well-loved teacher and designer) and edited by Dennis Sharp (1976). A book as fresh as the day it was compiled and with some exceptionally good photographs. Contemplating the pleasure of these pages, it would be a niggardly spirit that did not feel the sap rising and another spring not too far away ... A more straightforward example would be Robin Skelton's memorial vol-

ume to the critic and poet Herbert Read, forming (incidentally) a good general introduction to his work. (George Woodcock's *Herbert Read: the stream and the source* is worth offering as an alternative.)

9   Exhibits. This category, of books that have 'object-quality' is depressingly small. Any rigour of design consciousness is normally excluded from publishing. Some historical rarities appear in facsimile (e.g. the Bauhaus books). Examples still in circulation as originals will include *Der Stuhl* by Heinz and Bodo Rasch, Tschichold's *Typographische Gestaltung* (which it is instructive to compare with the later translated edition, *Asymmetric typography*), and the oddly charismatic *Flat book* by J. L. Martin and Sadie Speight. Among late entrants, there is work from Froshaug, from Sandberg (for the Stedelijk Museum, Amsterdam), and from Otl Aicher.

10   Evidential books (see 5). Books that present enough comparative evidence, on any matter of design concern, for the readers to make up their own minds (such evidence would normally include drawings and photographs). A thin entry might be expected here, and the type-form is scarce. Roth's *The new architecture* was a good one. Although confined to photographic evidence, the post-war *Domus* books just qualify. (On desks, fireplaces, kitchens, and so on.)

11   Essays and papers, short monographs. Usually topical, but not always ephemeral; for example Colin Rowe's 'The mathematics of the ideal villa' (*Architectural Review*, March 1947), now collected in book form. *Buildings and society* (edited by King) is a set of essays on 'the social development of the built environment'. Another example: Bruno Zevi's brief *The modern language of architecture*, which is a cheerful antidote to Jencks (see 27).

12   Course books. In the past few years the Open University has been building up course-and-source material of notable quality. Design students (in colleges) may not realize the useful availability of Course Units and Readers, with related audio- and video-tapes, film, and radio and TV programmes. Work by Nigel Cross and Tim and Charlotte Benton, for instance, is reliably first class. The nature of OU course-work has varied over the years, in response to public

demand and to internal policy-making. 'History of architecture and design 1890–1939' (A305) was a pioneering effort that generated valuable readers and course material. *Man-made futures*, edited by Cross, Elliott and Roy, is a useful anthology, produced for a now discontinued design methods course.

13   Related books. An elusive but potent category. Good examples have been Ruth Benedict's *Patterns of culture* and Jane Abercrombie's *Anatomy of judgement* – the first giving distance, the second, proportion, to any way of studying design. Design being a transactional art, it follows that the looser areas of behavioural psychology have a practical interest, despite the inability of most designers to 'place' such work confidently enough to form conclusions about it. At the sunnier end of the spectrum are books like the catchy *Games people play*, or moving along it a little, authors like Erving Goffman. Designers have always been interested in the Gestalt people – for obvious reasons – and holistic writers like L. L. Whyte have had a similar appeal. Where does a list of related books actually stop? Maybe such books can classify as repositories or tools; the former being heavy and soporific and seeming to sop up energy, like a hot bath; the latter helping to make good work seem worthwhile. A designer's books will (thus) be estimated by their effects.

14   Distant relations. Books that make connections, or present images of critical attitude, in ways likely to be useful. An open and personal category. Some might include *Zen and the art of motor cycle maintenance* (Robert Pirsig); others much prefer their maintenance manuals straight, with pictures. For the literary-minded, Terry Eagleton's *Literary theory* will startle and challenge readers who thought they knew a bit about it. By contrast, the poet Ezra Pound's *ABC of reading* is really a book for writers (and far from dull): arguably an excellent design primer. Title collectors will relish Donald Davie's *Articulate energy* – there is more within. George Steiner's *Language and silence* will not be read by design trendies; but should be.

15   Design philosophy and predicament books. Examples: Toffler's *Future shock*, Papanek's *Design for the real world*, and almost any

writing by Buckminster Fuller. For aphorisms in sharp focus: Frederic Samson's book of sayings, *Dotes and antidotes* (published by the Royal College of Art).

16   Design theory-and-practice. *What is a designer* is one such; John Christopher Jones' *Design methods* is an enduring and more specialized example. The latter-day Chris Alexander is tirelessly and biblically prescriptive in his series beginning with *The timeless way of building*; with Bachelard, a literary man's view of formal values.

17   Technical books generally. A mainstay of any designer's consultative reading. Too many and various to list or describe. Such books will be specified by course tutors.

18   Catalogues. Possibly a sub-set of 17 but rather different in kind and function, and often more ephemeral. There is no doubt that catalogues claim an unchallenged primacy in the field; some designers read little else. Catalogues may be related to the big trade exhibitions, or to wholesale distributive sources, or may be directly and concisely informative about a particular range of products. A few, like the Wilkes-Berger, are splendidly suggestive. It has been well said that any man in a tight spot will draw comfort from these pages; yet, it is not easy to describe the special satisfaction of well-presented ironmongery. Then there are the great catalogues; always, alas, of the past, and still to be chanced upon, occasionally, in country houses, or upon the bookshelves of retired shop-foremen. To scan these is to enter a lost world of mechanical authority; the steel engravings alone are of a privileged artistry. The Guillet machine catalogue might be spoken of in this context; but rarely seen. Catalogue systems are another thing altogether and appear under 20.

19   Definitive references. The major works, like Needham's *Science and civilisation in China*, or the big encyclopaedias, or the OED.

20   Common references. These include the technical reference systems, using CI / sfB classification (commercially serviced or run by the design office) and the standard reference books such as *Specification*. Less obvious are publications like *Which?* as a consumer

cheek on the retail market, and the small handy books (including diaries) that rank as pocket references. These might include (for instance) Matila Ghyka's useful *Geometrical composition and design*, or Charles Hayward's *Woodworkers pocket book*. For English-language purposes, designers may well use Chambers, Fowler, and Partridge (*Chambers twentieth century dictionary*, Fowler's *Dictionary of modern English usage*, and Partridge's *Usage and abusage*, respectively).

21   Books on education. Not all students are too keen to read about education while still in its grip; yet it is a proper function of any educative process to question itself and informed questioning is the best kind. Those who wish to take a critical backward look at their schooling might enjoy Reimer's *School is dead*, Goodman's *Compulsory miseducation*, and the irrepressible Ivan Illich's *Deschooling society*. A centre-view is provided by R. S. Peters (whose 'philosophy of education' is attacked from a Marxist angle by Pateman in *Counter course*) and by A. N. Whitehead's trenchant *Aims of education*. On the left the legendary fieldworker A. S. Neill has *Summerhill*; on the right are Cox and Rhodes Boyson in the Black Papers (not always quite as black as they sound), and perhaps Bantock.

22   Books on design education. Many omissions. For instance, it has been hard work to get the facts about the Hochschule für Gestaltung at Ulm. The international disturbances of 1968 have been well documented; for England see the Penguin *The Hornsey affair* and Tom Nairn in *The beginning of the end* (evidence from the other side appears in the Report from the Select Committee). Educational politics grind on remorselessly, with a few specialists attempting documentation and the occasional challenge. Gordon Lawrence and David Page attempted this in their essay in *A degree of choice* (edited by Finch and Rustin). The Bauhaus is now well covered: given a good library it is worth going to Wingler's *The Bauhaus*; failing which the Bayer/Gropius *Bauhaus* is probably the best short survey. There are now an increasing number of books on design education at secondary school level (a matter of interest to many students taking degree courses, apart from its intrinsic merit). An example, *Design education in schools*, is by Bernard Aylward, who pioneered the Leicester experiment, which combined course development with new school buildings adapted to it.

23   Magazines. British design (and design/architectural) magazines seem to proliferate endlessly; they are well enough known in college libraries and specialist shops; overseas equivalents will be found there too. It is less well observed that all trades have their magazines, and these are fruitful sources when required (even for their advertisements). Some magazines generate books out of special issues or series of contributions (the *Architectural Review*, for example). Among recent enterprises, the English *Form* was a welcome if brief visitant; worth looking for. Good magazines of a quite unconnected kind will sometimes have a run of a year or two when their quality is exceptionally high (and therefore of interest beyond the charmed circle of their ordinary readership) – this happened to the magazine *Anarchy* under the unobtrusive editorship of Colin Ward, and more recently (1979–80) the American *Wooden Boat*. It would be hard to connect these with each other, or either with a designer's normal interests (so watch out).

24   Bran tubs and oddities. These are books with something for everybody, and the *Whole Earth Catalog* is surely the most kaleidoscopic. This one is as hard to classify as it intends to be. An example of an 'oddity' (only by the present terms of reference) is *Richard's bicycle book* by Ballantine: handy for those with bicycles, obviously, but also exemplary for its illustrations (designers please note) and for the agreeably unpretentious – yet informative – nature of its discourse (other technical writers might note).

25   Alternative attitudes. Well-known examples are the diagnostic *Blueprint for survival* (by the editors of *The Ecologist*), and E. F. Schumacher's heartwarming *Small is beautiful* – with its sequels *A guide for the perplexed* and *Good work*. Fading, but not without interest are Roszak's *The making of a counter culture* and Guinness' reply to it *The dust of death*. Of constructive account beyond its strict subject-matter (housing) is John Turner's contribution as an activist and field-worker, brought together in his book *Housing by people*, putting the case, baldly speaking, for self-build and for the social principle of user-control. On a similar wavelength are books by the architect Colin Ward (e.g. *Vandalism* and *The child in the city*), who edited the *Bulletin of Environmental Education* and directed

the Schools Council's 'Art and the Built Environment' project. Mike Cooley, the shop-steward from Lucas Aerospace, provides a radical reappraisal of computer-aided design in *Architect or bee?* Women's movement contributions include *Making space* by the group Matrix, with a useful bibliography.

26 Alternative hardware. A rapidly growing collection of books on all aspects of 'loose fit, low energy, long life' (Alex Gordon's formulation, see *RIBA Journal*, January 1974) and how to do it in the design and building of devices, mechanisms, and environments of all kinds (what the motorcycle sidecar enthusiasts used to call 'the outfit'). As would be expected, advice ranges from the homely to the arcane, and from DIY technology to advanced engineering. Students wishing to study wind power or solar energy systems, for instance, will find a considerable literature awaiting them. Walter Segal's refreshingly down-to-earth designs for low-cost housing were reviewed in the *Architects' Journal* (and see the special memorial issue, 4.5.1988).

27 Anti-modern-movement. Currently as fashionable as plug-in technology was in the 1960s and taking one of two characteristic positions: the first, that there is an identifiable body of work now sufficiently considerable to be called 'post-modern' and that the 'modern movement' which it replaces may now be deemed a spent force; or the second, that the modern movement had no real warrant for the largeness of its claims, has got itself into a formal and philosophical cul-de-sac, and that this is consistent with the faulty premises of its origin. The first position is illustrated in various books by Charles Jencks (such as *The language of post-modern architecture*) and the second perhaps best by *Morality and architecture* by Watkin. This book and others similar are discussed in a critical symposium 'The edifice crumbles' (*Architectural Review*, February 1978) to which interested readers may wish to refer. The controversy is less simplistic than the above summary might suggest, but somewhat scholastic in tone and stylistic in its central interest. The anti-design writers are far more radical, and having rejected the design profession as it currently professes, are more concerned to adduce alternative attitudes (see 25). Their rejection follows from the view that

decision-making generally in the community needs to be deprofessionalized, involving far more user-participation than is now the case, and that designers (when their concerns are not wholly trivial) may in the end do more harm than good. Turner and Ward seem on the whole to take this view, though it is entailed by their position rather than central to it. Malcolm MacEwan's *Crisis in architecture*, easy to group with the writings of those who decry the modern movement, is in fact a perennial reminder, and in this case a constructive one, that all is not well at the RIBA.

This completes the suggested *range* of possibly useful design reading, without closing the door on late comers, new arrivals, or other likely entrants. It must be said once more, however, that for a pot, a building, a rug, or even a well-baked loaf of bread, no amount of reading will take the place of touch, sight, taste, sound, and smell; by which token it should be added that the only reliable form of words is a poem, and possibly a novel – all other forms being insufficiently transparent. We read criticism to increase our enjoyment of these things, to understand them, and perhaps to make them better. They are, after all, leavings.

As to the modern movement and how is it doing, the answer this book gives is – not very nicely thank you, but as well as can be expected, taking everything into account. Designers do, for practical reasons, inhabit a house of theory of their own; it concentrates their minds or helps to. These notes have been concerned to open doors and windows, and to welcome guests. The structure is surely a makeshift one, draughty, and unsure in its foundations. This is true of all such structures since Hiroshima and the concentration camps: the extremes of contemporary reference.

It used to he said that to keep sane, modern man must either come to know God, or be in permanent urgent conference with Marx, Freud, and Einstein, or come to an arrangement with the Devil and go into business. Few designers have lost themselves wholeheartedly in any one of these alternatives – if they had any serious interest in the modern movement. Perhaps they should have done, and perhaps they failed to learn deeply enough the lessons of dematerialization, the 'reductio ad absurdum' of their reductionism; being thus neither scientific enough nor religious enough.

After all, Beethoven, who on any sensible estimate of 'the present' must still be accounted our greatest contemporary, made matters plain in his late piano music (and perhaps in the quartets for those who have caught up with them). W. J. Turner wrote an interesting little book to adduce the view that 'all art is the imagination of love, and music is the imagination of love *in sound*'. The parallel suggestion is that 'well-doing' in Lethaby's sense is the play of love upon inert material; the finding of its forms – to which the clarifying tasks of our epoch, the finding of each other, and the conversion of mass into energy and relationship, are contributory. In a situation of physical entanglement (the world of the transactional) there are two images of correspondence to such tasks: that of definition, the 'area of concern', and that of conduction, 'energy striking through' (the through-and-through requirement of modern design, which gives a characteristically figure to ground situation in which the perimeter or frame is unacceptable). Christians who happen to read these lines, or between them, will immediately see what is implied: it is indeed possible to argue that the modern movement 'an sich' was and is a making-straight the path of the Lord; is about and around some implications of that task; and that where it fails is always the mark of secular presumption. It is amusing to think how such a speculation might be received in some quarters. Related studies, the concern of this part, might wish to endorse or to dismiss such a claim – but in either case by their fruits let them be judged; for such studies will only be helpful if response is quickened, and life and love allowed to become more abundant. It is well known that where apathy dwells, comes the evil day.

Categories, however, are clusters, and this part will end with a linear connection. It is a cheerful one, and demonstrates a further dimension of critical resource in the modern movement. If it can be argued – as indeed it can – that the history of consciousness is a chain of hands, then our situation demands that the hands we seek shall be neither flabby, evasive, nor treacherous. 'Good with their hands.' Where shall we look?

Among the founding fathers of the modern movement, which description must include William Morris pre-eminently, let us begin with his friend and contemporary the great Peter Kropotkin, author of *Mutual aid: a factor of evolution* and the prescient *Fields, factories and workshops* (re-edited by Colin Ward). Kropotkin (1842–1921) was a source of inspiration both to Patrick Geddes (1854–1932) and later to Lewis Mumford (1895–1990). In the first decades of this century there are three writers – all active and substantial men – who might be said to stand for the concerns discussed here: Geddes, Ashbee, and Lethaby, who were approximate contemporaries. Geddes, splendid man that he was, is usefully appraised through Paddy Kitchen's biographical study *A most unsettling person* (there is a lengthier book by Boardman). He was a synthesizer of ideas and a social activist, much concerned with user-participation; in which regard it must be clear that men like John Turner and Pat Crooke (or Illich) stand within the tradition of concern of the modern movement, and not, as some might suggest, outside it. Ashbee said of Geddes 'his work has ever a touch of prophecy' and 'when all's said and done … his prophecy is likely to sound the farthest'. It is interesting and rather unexpected that he found no hesitation in commending Mackintosh for his Glasgow School of Art, saying 'the real artist is he who, like Mackintosh in the Art College of Glasgow (one of the most important buildings in Europe) gets his effects within the sternest acceptances of modern conditions. For here never was concrete more concrete, steel more steely …'

Ashbee (1863–1942) was an interesting man whose concern with the workshop concept, and what might be done with it, is perhaps not as well known as it should be. (See his *Craftsmanship in competitive industry*, an account of the problems faced by his Guild and School of Handicraft [founded 1888] in moving from London's East End to Chipping Campden.) He was, as Pevsner implies, no intellectual Luddite and stated in *Should we stop teaching art?* (1911) that 'Modern civilization rests on machinery, and no system for the endowment, or the encouragement, of the teaching of art can be sound that does not recognize this' – a shift both from Morris and from his own earlier position when he spoke with rather more reserve: 'we do not reject the machine, we welcome it. But we desire to see it mastered …'

Lethaby (1857–1931) is in some ways a larger and more recognizable figure, partly because of his contribution to design education as Principal of the Central School of Arts & Crafts in London, and as a Professor at the Royal College of Art; but better, perhaps, for the vigour and clarity of his writing, of which his book of essays *Form in civilization*, reprinted in 1957 with an introduction by Lewis Mumford, is an excellent example. Lethaby seems to gain in stature as he recedes into history. He has been called a moralist (is this a human failing? he was certainly no prude or killjoy) but he is better seen as a realist, impatient with aestheticism and what Mumford calls 'the shams and sophistications that Lethaby loathed'; always, however, with a moral dimension at the core of his thinking. Here are some characteristic aphorisms:

Art is a natural human aptitude which has been explained almost
    out of existence.
The task of civilization is to add to what may be loved.
He owns most who loves most.
To live on the labour of others is a kind of cannibalism.
There are too many professional men, tradesmen and noblemen:
    too few men.

Lewis Mumford finally met Geddes in 1923, finding him (as was common) extremely difficult, though his presence 'shook my life to the core'. Mumford himself became one of the wisest synoptic writers of our time, influencing (together with Giedion) several generations of design and architectural students through his books *Technics and civilization*, *The culture of cities* and *The condition of man*. He was a good friend to students and designers who search continually below 'the surface of the face of things' for the meaning of our time, and how they should best respond to its demands.

Mumford wrote from America; in Britain, probably the last critic of the breadth and sensibility to carry forward this tradition was the poet and essayist and polymath Herbert Read (1893–1968), who has already been mentioned for his book *Art and industry*. Read, who was also a follower of Kropotkin – more explicitly so than Mumford – wrote widely on the arts, philosophy, sociology and literature. His substantial contribution *Education through art*, which did so much to influence British primary school teaching, was warmly admired by Walter Gropius. Read's personal impact upon British cultural life is no longer well remembered – he is too near – but in his modest and seemingly tireless way he continuously urged and promoted an awareness of modern art and design (and literature) that was slow in coming to these insular shores from the Continent and America.

Here, then, are joined hands from Kropotkin through Geddes, Ashbee, and Lethaby, to Mumford and Read, and on to E. F. Schumacher and others like Colin Ward and Paul Goodman; and here, observably, is a tradition of warmth and human concern in a critical culture, linked at every point to the growth of the modern movement, and emphasizing its roots in the necessary thinking of the twentieth century in respect to its complex inheritance. It would be tedious to develop this indication – it is no more – into possible cross-connections, which it may interest students to do; nor should a world of social imperatives be found coterminous with that of nuts and bolts and object-making, the 'traditions' for which are outside the scope of this book to examine. However, Instant Trend and Moneyman (and other television stereotypes) must be contained in their redefining of our culture. Those who are exasperated by the confusion of stylistic trivia with the spirit and attitudes of the modern movement, which are the source of its relevance, might draw encouragement from some of the sources mentioned. For my part, these are hands I would take in complete confidence. Like the poor (it seems), what is modern is always with us; and open to transformation. Here is Herbert Read's poem 'A song for the Spanish anarchists':

> The golden lemon is not made
>   but grows on a green tree:
> A strong man and his crystal eyes
>   is a man born free.
>
> The oxen pass under the yoke
>   and the blind are led at will:
> But a man born free has a path of his own
>   and a house on the hill.
>
> And men are men who till the land
>   and women are women who weave;
> Fifty men own the lemon grove
>   and no man is a slave.

93

8   Summary: students as designers

Students who want to be useful in the world, who see chaos and want order, who lack self-confidence, and who are swamped by the apparently required armoury of skills and facts, are sometimes rashly seduced by unitary views of disparate phenomena – it seems hopeful that way, and it seems manageable. Those who court lateral thinking to infinity can easily arrive at the semantic double-think in which concrete equals abstract; an achievement which some design theorists have managed effortlessly. Many a pretty paradox can flourish, and indeed be artfully cultivated, in a society that lacks a spiritual dynamic, and would like the best of east and west without the penalties of either.

Design has a very broad spectrum of opportunities that can be made socially worthwhile. Some are mechanical, some ephemeral, some interpretive, some call upon unique solutions, some move toward those generalized type-forms that Gropius talked about. Designers themselves are equally various in personal make-up. The first task for a student is to know – and accept – himself. The second is to educate himself (and here, because the word 'himself' has special weight, it is a relief to break the language convention – a problem throughout this book – and add herself); accepting formal education as one set of constraints and opportunities exercised within the temporary benefits of community. Remembering, in this matter of education, a saying by Robert Graves – that it is easier and more common to hate hypocrisy than to love the truth. The third task is to sense out, quite intimately, a growing sense of accomplishment that is accessible simultaneously to eye, hand, reason, and imagination; testing each ground to spring from.

This is not an original specification for survival. The point to reiterate is that so few survive at the level of creative expectancy that formal education generates – and to which subsequent experience adds, too frequently, a tepid aftermath. As things are, the one thing about the future of which a student can be sure, is that its demands on him are strictly unpredictable: the rough shape of possibilities may be discernible, but the exact and tangible nature of a creative challenge is a happening and not a forecast.

How, then, to keep open to the future with enough personal acumen and buoyancy to cope with its opportunities at full stretch? If students feel blocked by society as it is, then they must help find constructive ways forward to a better one. In a personal way, the question must be answered by individual students in their own terms, but as far as design goes, it is possible to see two slippery snakes in the snakes and ladders game. The first snake is to suppose that the future is best guaranteed by trying to live in it; and the second is an assumption that must never go unexamined – that the required tools of method and technique are more essential than spirit and attitude. This snake offers a sterility that reduces the most 'correct' procedures to a pretentious emptiness, whether in education or in professional practice.

The danger is reinforced by another consideration. There can be a certain hollowness of accomplishment known to a student in his own heart, but which he is obliged to disown, and to mask with considerations of tomorrow, merely to keep up with the pressures surrounding him. Apart from the success-criteria against which his work may be judged, there is a more subtle and pervasive competitiveness from which it is difficult to be exempt, even by the most sophisticated exercises in detachment. Hence the importance of recognizing that education is a fluid and organic growth of understanding, or it is nothing. Similarly, when real participation is sidestepped, and education is accepted lovelessly as a hand-out, then reality can seem progressively more fraudulent.

Fortunately, the veriest beginner can draw confidence from the same source as a seasoned design specialist, once it is realized that the foundations of judgement in design, and indeed the very structure of decision, are rooted in ordinary life and in human concerns, not in some quack professionalism with a degree as a magic key to the mysteries. From then on, to keep the faith, to keep open to the future, is to know the present as a commitment in depth, and to know the past where its spirit can still reach us. As to know your enemy is more usefully to know, and to seek, your friends. The enemy can usually be trusted to reveal himself (or is only too easy to manufacture).

A designer comes to recognize that his world is only fleetingly conjectural. Just as a student finds it hard to believe that anyone will actually give him a job – and there he is five years later, working and still managing to eat – so it is with all our legendary tomorrows: they offer their problems concretely enough, if we are there, and refuse to take no for an answer. It is also true that a designer interprets reality through the modalities of action; in the end, his work stands or falls by the intractably objective qualities of an outcome. Only in such good sense is he a philosopher: in making actual an experience of design, and thus constantly redefining what the word (and the work) stand for. Yet because we occupy our differing roles only in virtue of our common predicament, which is our humanity, there is no end to the questions we must continue to ask.

Design is thus simultaneously a realm of values and a matter of engrossingly particular decisions, many of which are highly technical. There is a threshold up to which we can quantify, and this is often enough the task for a professional: less an equation of meaning than one of ordered evidence. Beyond this threshold, design is strictly a cultural option. It always has been. We humble ourselves, we sharpen our wits, and we offer, at the very least, our moments of lucidity. Our concern is always 'the place of value in a world of facts', but there is no role waiting for us, there is merely the chance of making one out of the sheer courage of our perceptions. In the same way, if you want to link hands with the spirit of the modern movement, it won't come to meet you; you must go out and make it your own.

9 Explanation

The change of paper identifies the reference area of this book, and
should make it easy of access. Although the notes may be consulted
separately under their headings, the key parts are 10 and 11 ('How
is design work done?' and 'Communication for designers'), which
put the rest into context. A simplified overall picture is the first
requirement. The detail can be filled in by experience, or – when
needed – from the more specialized textbooks. For this reason, and
to keep the whole thing manageable, the notes are kept to basics
and essentials. If the practical advice and check-lists are prefaced
by general discussion, the advice will be found restated in tabular
form at the end of the part. Where more specialized work is touched
upon (for example, that of a surveyor in relation to the survey notes
given in part 14) the advice is reduced to considerations that all
designers will find essentially reasonable. At a more general level,
some aspects of diagnostic technique are seldom given the attention
they deserve, and will seem unfamiliar for that reason; for instance
the brief notes on 'Asking questions' may seem quite difficult to
anyone without training in the field. Practice becomes the answer.

It is hard to strike a balance between professional realism, and
the more personal and informal design situations. 'How is design
work done?' gives too simple a picture for building design, yet is
far too elaborate for textiles or ceramics. However, designers must
know how things happen in the ordinary commercial world; the
conventions employed, and the order of events as normally experienced – whether in lesser or greater detail. It is against the demands
of the transactional world that technique has to be evaluated. There
is also some correspondence between 'the way things go' and the
various possible logical models of the design process, which (when
they work) may offer some help in allocating effort where it is most
needed.

This matter is discussed in part 5, 'Problems with method', and
is further examined here – in a practical way – in parts 11 to 16
inclusive. However, the recommendations are chiefly concerned to

develop technique in harmony with understanding, and stop well short of any more systematic view of design methodology. The difference may be seen on a rough-and-ready workshop analogy, for which 'method' would represent an overall strategy for all cases, how things are best put together and in what order; 'technique' being what tools to select, how to keep them sharp, and how to use them. Both have their place, but in a workshop sharp tools are the first requirement. Both are most appreciated after mistakes have repeatedly occurred and much time and energy been seen to be wasted (on the workshop analogy, from muddle and from blunt tools). Thus students may find these notes a bore, or a mystification, in the first year, but thereafter and progressively, they should prove helpful. As is so well known in sports training – or in any serious pursuit of high standards – technique is hard work, and this is inescapable; there are no short cuts. What of method?

Since the 1960s many design schools have experimented with different aspects of problem-solving disciplines and with systematic design method. Before 1968 – a useful watershed – substantial work had come from the Hochschule für Gestaltung at Ulm. In Britain there had been notable published work from Bruce Archer and John Christopher Jones. David Warren Piper surfaced at Hornsey College of Art during the troubles, with some interesting work. My own contribution at the Royal College of Art had to do with diagnostic technique, and communication methods, briefly summarized here. Chris Alexander wrote the suggestive *Notes on the synthesis of form* and Jane Abercrombie her very useful *The anatomy of judgement* and many papers on learning and teaching derived from her research programme at the Bartlett School of Architecture and elsewhere. In America, the prestigious Buckminster Fuller was still soldiering on, in pursuit of global strategies for survival and an 'anticipatory design capability' to put them into effect.

Since 1968, designers have tended to take a less messianic and more piecemeal view of their social role, with a bit less confidence in the grand strategy. This is perhaps reflected in methodological studies, which apart from advance in the field of CAD (Computer Aided Design) have been concerned with retrenchments and reappraisals. The matter was nicely summarized by Nigel Cross of the Open University in his 'An introduction to design methods' (*Infor-*

mation Design Journal, vol. 1, no. 4, 1980), which has a useful set of references. Interested students should also consult J.C. Jones' *Design methods*. For a more detailed account of professional practice and office procedure, see Dorothy Goslett's *The professional practice of design* and Ron Green's *Architect's guide to running a job*. J.B. Creswell's classic *Honeywood file* is a cautionary tale: very amusing, readable, and instructive.

10 How is design work done?

Much design work is carried out in a very direct and informal way. The degree of formality becomes a function of scale and the number of interests represented. Of course an artisan designer (of any kind) works very directly and with a minimum of 'communication procedures'. As was explained in part 1, however, this book takes a middle-range view of design opportunities and here matters of procedural technique become critical, for reasons given in the following parts.

The step-by-step account of events that follows is intended to place design procedure in its normal context for (say) the design of the interior of a small department store, in this case to include some structural work, all fitments, and graphics; or that of a large exhibition, which would be comparable. The sequence is 'normal' for present purposes, but naturally there are variants.

From such an account it is possible to abstract out an analytical model of the design process, and thus to see what is irreducible over a wider range of problems. This would merely confuse the descriptive purpose of these notes, but readers are directed to methodological references (see part 9) for a systematic view in such terms.

The procedures show the designer approaching an unknown situation, making himself familiar with it, taking instructions, making sure they are fully understood, weighing the possibilities, discussing them, arriving at conclusions, offering proposals, modifying them, providing drawings and other instructions to a third party, and supervising the outcome. The result is something new in the world; a product, an environmental change; a new set of possibilities. In dynamic balance to effect this change are the interests of four persons or groups of people: the owner or client or employer (the word client is used because, for the designer, it is the least ambiguous); the user or public or consumer; the designer plus any technical advisers; and the contractor or manufacturer. Each party deploys social resources in a different way and there is no parity of representation between these interests; that of the larger one (the user or public) often being, in effect, mute. There is, however, an on-going economic relationship between the client and his market or public, which has to some extent its own system of checks and balances: the designer and contractor come into the situation briefly as agents of change, with the designer most potently concerned with its nature. His responsibility is therefore a complex one: is he working for himself, for God ('good work'), the client, the builder or manufacturer, the public or user, or in some embracing respect the interests of society as a whole? He may feel that the resources available (labour, skills, materials, and including the special skills of his client and his own professional training) are a social resource, and that their effective control through money at the disposal of the client, is largely an arbitrary matter; that his role is simply to free and 'optimize' an outcome as best he can; or he may take the view that his direct contractual responsibility is to his client's personal interests which he is called upon to serve, and all else must be so governed. The designer must be aware of the highly contingent nature of all his decisions in these respects; he must also remember that each possibility is a new one.

1   Letter or telephone call from client or equivalent
Arrange a meeting at his and your convenience.

2   Meet client
This is an unpredictable occasion, though the client will usually be anxious to convince himself that you are competent, experienced, personable, and able to look after his interests. Prepare accordingly. If you decide to take some work, a vast and shapeless portfolio may prove damaging by making the client feel that you are setting the pace, and in doing so, exploiting his own lack of technical expertise. Equally it is unwise to turn up with batteries of assistants, tape-recorders, and measuring tapes, etc. It is most essential to *listen* properly, and to take notes; listening being that part of conversation that a designer must practise and get word-perfect. Briefs; see 15.

3   Visit site, meet other interested parties
This is again an informal occasion – not a site survey – but an important one, because first impressions are important. Note them. The

'parties' may be the clients (plural) or the client's business associates. Take camera, but only use if the occasion seems suitable.

4   Exchange of letters (leading to contract or letters of contract)
Must be considered in formal terms; free of too many references to 'I', and not overburdened by design jargon or unsuccessful attempts to sound like a business man (e.g. 'the favour of your letter' and 'may we assure you of our best attention at all times'). The best form usually is a direct and friendly letter, practical and reserved in tone, with facts or lists separated out as an accompanying sheet, such that the client can hand this round without his colleagues having to work through the more ephemeral or personal bits. At the beginning of a design job, it is often helpful to a client to have a very simple account of the design sequence that you usually follow, so the client knows what to expect and roughly when to expect it. Be careful, however, unless the job is one you have encountered before. A letter is a good vehicle for this simple information. You should advise a client that consultants may be necessary (engineer, quantity surveyor, etc.) and you should make him aware that formal consents may be involved, and that it may be necessary to consider his personal insurances, his obligations of tenancy, the rights of adjoining properties, planning and fire office consents, and (in the case of an exhibition) the exhibition regulations.

   Obviously, correspondence continues to the sweet or bitter end of the design process.

5   Contract or letter of contract
Legal documents, highly conventionalized. Should be separately studied as an aspect of 'professional practice', the subtleties of which are outside our present terms of reference.

6   Letters of record or enquiry to other interested parties
Such letters will always be short and to the point – such letters are almost conventions and most of them go into the filing records of local authorities, etc.

7   Site and premises survey, subsequently drawn up
It will save endless work if this is done properly because the draw-

ings must be very accurate descriptions of fact, accompanied by photographs, recordings if necessary, and extensive notes. Sometimes you will employ a surveyor to produce the measured drawing; you will still need your own observations for design purposes. See part 14, 'Survey before plan'.

8 Questions

The asking of questions, and finding the right ones to ask, is fundamental to such dignity and relevance as a designer's role can conceivably possess; this process is no conjuring act or trick of the trade with intent to deceive; on the contrary, the purpose of questioning is to identify and solicit such truths as may be available. See part 15, 'Asking questions'. Here, it should merely be noted that questions may be asked orally, in which case it is sometimes acceptable at this stage to use a tape recorder, or questions may be submitted rather more formally as a questionnaire. Questions will include requests for factual information available to the client (e.g. for a shop, very elaborate questions about stock and sales policy). It is unwise to ask questions casually by letter or at random meetings. The client will usually respond well to carefully prepared questions; they are a measure of your concern for his interests.

9 Research, permissions, consultation

This will involve a consultation of all other parties or interests involved, particularly local authorities in the form of the district surveyor, fire and health officers, etc, together with all necessary technical information (catalogues, etc.) and anything else necessary to complete your reference data. There may at this stage be any relevant form of public consultation, which can occur through representative bodies or pressure groups, or by the summoning of meetings, or by taking samples of local opinion, or by the more controlled 'opinion poll' method, or by seeking available evidence from past experience. It is doubtful if any of these approaches would be employed for the scale of work under discussion (though they could be), but it is necessary to mention them here. Research and consultation is a considerable and continuing task and is not neatly confined to this stage of the job.

10 Sizing up the job

At this stage you should have enough information to work out an office programme with a clear allocation of personal responsibilities for the conduct of the job. This exercise will give you an intuitive idea of the possibilities latent in the design work (conditioned by time, money, and the nature of the problem) and just how far you can afford to develop them. This will affect your whole subsequent approach; your personal strategy.

11 Preliminary ideas

Design begins here in a formal sense, though you may by now have a design concept or a 'mental set' from your first meeting with the client or your first view of the site (this is a matter of experience). Mistrust mental sets until they have proved their relevance. This is the stage at which ideas are roughed out diagrammatically and working principles examined, tested, and agreed. Such ideas may take a mainly visual form (but will usually be diagrammatic in character) or, if you use a 'report' as a kind of developing discussion with yourself, may be verbal argument accompanied by concept diagrams. It is difficult to generalize about the thinking that may go on at this stage.

12 Report

A report is not always necessary, but it is a most valuable instrument for two-way consultation. See part 16, 'Reports and report writing'. The report will embody your proposals in principle and your reasons for suggested courses of action. The report may include diagrams and a plan layout, and may include catalogues and other references. The report should *not* commit you to what the job may finally look like. You should normally include a discussion of alternatives, for three reasons: to show why your proposal is the best one (as it should be), to make it clear that all possibilities have been adequately canvassed, and to gain 'reasonable assent' to what you propose, which is best done in an open contemplation of the options. On the other hand, it is unwise to present evenly balanced alternatives, unless you are really convinced that it is right to do so (your client may think, 'what the hell am I paying him for?'). The report is not a brief, however. One of its purposes is to focus discussion, and another, to bring to light new considerations which your client, or other interested parties, may not have thought of hitherto; finally, its purpose most succinctly, is to make the definition of a brief securely possible, and less liable to be faulted. Always remember therefore that a report is a consultation document.

13 Pause: recipients consider your report, copies of which you may have sent by post or presented personally.

14 Meetings, conversations, etc: to discuss the report and your client's reactions to it.

15 Brief
A 'brief' is a statement of your agreed terms of reference for developing a design to presentation stage. In a small or simple job the brief will emerge much earlier, in correspondence with your client. Here, the brief emerges from final agreement after the report has been fully discussed, with all modifications taken into account. It is highly desirable to set out your brief in a manner that obviates any kind of misunderstanding, but it is by no means an onerous task (not comparable in length or scope or detail with a report). Its purpose is to reassure the client that all his reservations have not been brushed aside, and to remind him that from now on work must be seriously under way without his interference. This is the last chance for the client to reject your approach to his problem (unless he finds your presentation drawings unacceptable).

16 Development
Here begins 'design' in the wholly conventional sense. You will have a model from your survey; if not, make one now. According to the nature of the job, you will proceed on the drawing board, in the layout pad, and in your workshop (if you have one) examining and developing ideas and testing them against your problem analysis if you have one as such, or against the reference data you have accumulated from your client and other sources (or against your report if you used the report as an analytical tool). You will discuss alternatives with trade representatives, with your quantity surveyor if you have one, with any relevant local authorities, and you will

form a good idea of the cost involved. All this will lead to a 'presentation' of your ideas, or rather your intentions, to the client.

17   Presentation

This will normally involve a model, sample sheets, diagrams, notes, sketches or 'perspectives', graphic layouts in whatever form appropriate, and will be personally 'presented' and argued for by yourself to the client or more usually to his board of directors. You may need an assistant, and, if it is a combined graphic-construction job, both of you will be present. A design presentation should go pleasantly enough if the work outlined above has been carried out properly. A presentation should be seen in definite terms (if it is inescapable) and any alternative ideas should merely be supporting evidence for your proposals.

18   Modifications

Certain changes may be necessary in the light of your client's response to the design presentation. Normally, such changes can be agreed informally (covered by letters) in your own office, and will not involve the effort of a further presentation.

19   Working drawings

The largest task now begins. Working drawings, or construction drawings, are detailed accurate informative *instructions* on which the work will be carried out. This is too complex to discuss here, except to say that drawings for consent will normally be done first, and the remaining bulk of the drawings must be carefully planned for the intended contractor or subcontractor or manufacturer. Drawings may be submitted to a quantity surveyor in order to receive a bill of quantities (a measured account of all labour and material items involved in the job) or may join a written specification and schedule in submission to competitive tender. These are technical matters which need not worry you in this short summary. Discussions with contractors may involve many modifications as the work proceeds, but if the contractor is unknown (i.e. to be decided by tender) such modifications will ensue after the contract has been settled.

20 Tender
Designers (in this case, as distinct from architects) will often work
in an informal way with a contractor already well known; in which
case much of this procedure loses its worrying aspects, but inescapably, however the job is done, a very large number of drawings must
reach the contractor with sufficient notes or verbal description (as
in a specification) to leave no room for doubt. (A specification de-
scribes in words the quality of materials, workmanship, etc, and
otherwise complements drawn information.) Students may hardly
be concerned with these procedures and this part of the working
sequence has been simplified accordingly.

21 Contractor begins work

22 Site supervision
This is an important part of design procedure. Even with the best
will in the world, and a very good set of drawings, things will always
go wrong on site and last-minute alterations will be essential. The
designer must also make sure that deliveries are properly in hand.
It is best to confine site instructions to the site foreman acting as
a general co-ordinator. Visits will also be necessary to the joinery
shop, to the printers or typesetters or indeed to any supplier or
subcontractor.

23 Payment
The designer will normally certify contractor's claims for submission to the client. In the case of shop-fitting or similar work, an
agreed proportion is held back for a six months 'defect liability
period'. Design fees will often be regulated (in a purely advisory way)
by national professional bodies.

24 Inspection at completion stage, and subsequently after any de-
fects are corrected.

25 Final settlement of finance and records. Photography. Filing
and storing of records. Job over.

NB It is rash to assume that the final relieved handshake is 'terminal' to a job – as newcomers will soon discover.

The above account is too tidy and logical, and has some rather alarming simplifications. In practice, constant new factors upset the brief, confusing or enriching it, and every kind of contingency will disturb a logical sequence. The design process is anyway a continuous interplay of creative thinking with reference data. However, in jobs of any substantial scale something like this apparent sequence is the only way to uncover the creative possibilities and to realize them. It will be seen that 'communication' becomes of first importance, with every new situation making its own quite distinct demands.

11   Communication for designers

Here, we shall discuss the ways and means of sending and receiving and getting information relevant to a purpose in hand, that purpose being the whole conduct of the design process as it affects a designer, his colleagues, the clients for whom he works, the contractor or manufacturer, the user or public, and all other parties or interests involved. This is a laboured definition, but it must be clear that here is purposeful communication used as a means – not an end – in situations of which the outlines are fairly well known. Graphic designers can find this confusing because their 'end' may be to find ways of transmitting a given message effectively. Thus they are using, in the design process, two lines of communication that may either cross or reinforce each other. Other students will be confused by the general tendency of design school drawings, reports, etc, to become in themselves an end rather than a means. It is very necessary to remind students that they will have formed an optimistic impression of the time normally available for design decisions, whether in a design office or in a hard-pressed workshop.

The most cursory study of the events that configure the 'design process' will reveal that effective communication is of their nature. Very many forms and procedures are involved whereby clients are questioned, research is carried out, information is sifted and stored, matters are discussed and intentions aired or confirmed, designs are initiated and developed, and action made appropriate by laborious processes of instruction.

An experienced designer will call upon experience; but will find it useful to ask certain questions as he prepares a drawing, writes a letter, or considers the scale and purpose of a model. The following notes place such questions in their context and suggest something of their nature; though until the evidence has been experienced or at least examined in some detail, it is wise to approach any procedural suggestions with some caution. It is not a formula that is required; merely, at this stage, a few guiding considerations.

Looking to the job sequence as evidence, it will be clear that the designer 'communicates' with himself – he exteriorizes his own thinking in drawings or, say, in using a report to think with – and with his colleagues in ways that may be highly personal, yet will have to assume recognizable conventions to the extent that some external response, or feedback, is called for. As the work moves away from him so must his chosen means become precise, until, finally, his instructions to a contractor must be entirely free of ambiguity. Yet a survey drawing, done at the beginning of a job, must be equally matter-of-fact. Again, there is no hard-and-fast distinction between words and drawings, and even while setting out a survey drawing a designer will be thinking in words about the drawing itself and the physical situation of which the drawing is an abstracted analogue. Is it possible, then to do more than feel one's way into an appropriate course of action?

To answer this question, it is necessary to see what is typically achieved by communication methods at every stage of the design process, and then to decide which procedures to use, and how any alternatives might affect the outcome.

Design methodology can usefully borrow from medicine a distinction between diagnostic and prescriptive procedures, though only a design consultant operates in so Olympian a spirit; the ordinary designer goes on to administer the medicine and thus combines the functions of nurse, chemist, and almoner in ensuring his patient's full recovery. Anyway, the idea of diagnosis and prescription is helpful. Broadly speaking, diagnostic work involves the classical apparatus of problem analysis, in greater or less degree according to the complexity of the job, and to the extent that the job does, in fact, constitute a 'problem'. (It is a mistake to suppose that all design jobs are best understood as problem-solving.) In the context we have used as an illustration, there will be three stages of diagnosis:

1   finding out: to observe, measure, assess, question and record – to get the facts and sense impressions which enable

2   sorting: to compare, distinguish, relate, and order the phenomena with which the designer is confronted, to 'unscramble' the mix and to find sets or categories which helpfully accomplish this

3   interpreting: to evaluate the situation thus exposed, to examine its potential in terms of means, effort, scale, kind, and so forth; to adduce the principles and the alternatives on which a prescriptive solution might be based.

Anyone who credits these procedures with 'objectivity' should realize that human judgement will colour and pre-select every seemingly objective assessment other than measurable fact reducible to number (and even here strange things can happen). Problem analysis would be a dull and fruitless affair if this were not so. All the more reason, then, for scruple, and for technique. Returning to the analogy with medicine, signs are more easily detected than symptoms. A designer who approaches his task with the single-mindedness of an adding machine must expect a barren diagnosis and often a misleading one. Imagination and empathy are as necessary as keen observation; to use a different vocabulary, the designer has to put himself out to meet the new situation with all his faculties as a human being, not merely shelter behind the privilege of his role-function (shielded by what is expected of him).

Technique is simply 'taking account of the other' in a realistic and effective way; since design is (at best) a socially transactional art (at worst just a transaction) this is necessary. For most people, and in most situations, there is no tidy linear sequence leading to an optimal design 'solution'. If this were the case, then all tidy-minded people would be, in principle, gifted designers. Often a diagrammatic answer may be available by these means – an answer that just covers the facts with a little to spare – and this is not to be despised. At least the client's existence and situation have been recognized. The quality of a design will grow out of the acuity and richness of response that a designer can bring to the opportunities confronting him, and this is a very personal matter; yet, it is also supra-personal in depending upon a relationship in depth between the designer and the full terms of reference for the work in hand. Technique helps all this to happen, not only by unfolding the possibilities and bringing them to light, but by involving the designer's enthusiasm in the process. Spirit and attitude are worth the larger part of logical method, in design practice as in design education.

It remains true that any design hypothesis will require a test-bed for its viability, misdirected effort must be minimized in this, because if there is one thing that design students are sold short on, it is an awareness of the time available for all these things. There is also a tendency for drawings to acquire the false status of end-products (this is worth repeating) whereas a practising designer's drawings are simply means to a given end, with a time limit for their completion.

Because the purpose of any given communication will not be terminal, but part of a network of interchanges of extremely various nature, the occasion or context must never be left out of account; it is not sufficient to think of a simple loop diagram with feedback. Information circuitry is as useful, and as misleading, as conceptual models of the design process in other terms: the dangers are, inhibited response, a false sense of 'objectivity' in procedures, rigidly estimated criteria, and a diminished sense of reality in a designer's informal relation to his work. Although such hazards can be described with some subtlety in cybernetic terms, there is no evidence that an acquaintance with information theory helps to bring home the bacon, in the range of opportunities discussed in this book – and some evidence that reliance upon it will produce a bag of bones. Students must unravel this matter for themselves.

The suggestions that follow are a simple way of selecting tools (and sharpening them) in the workshop of the mind. The use of four words is required:

mode: way in which a thing is done, class of thinking or intention exhibited – might be persuasive or informative, analytical or descriptive, interpretive, literal, final, provisional, open or closed as regards conventions, etc.

vehicle: known form or apparatus of communication, recognizable by conventions – might be a perspective drawing, a diagram, a report, a questionnaire, etc.

medium: physical means employed – might be card, cartridge paper, graph paper, wire, perspex, etc.

agent: instrumental means, tool or process – might be pen, computer and printer, photocopier, tape, duplicating machine, etc.

The following short statement puts the matter in a nutshell and suggests a simple way of evaluating any communication opportunity involving sender and receiver.

Design for designing
: the ins and outs of effective communication

Communication for designers:

is	purposeful (leads to or qualifies action in a design context)
is not	random, speculative, a work of art, self-contained, self-justifying
though	creativity may be so-prompted, so-ordered, and so-experienced
and	this will be obvious in communicating with yourself;
does	therefore, normally presuppose a knowable context, sender, receiver
for which	'context' implies interaction (more than two-way occurrences);
should	use and transmit energy economically;
and	in the forms (vehicles, conventions) that are used
must therefore be	clear, full, simple, direct, necessary, and acceptable (check)
unless	your purpose is better effected otherwise

NB   an 'acceptable' document employs the right tone of voice for receiver and purpose (this goes for physical character – layout, choice of materials, etc – as much as syntax and choice of words) for a drawing to be acceptable, its purpose must be estimated with precision, and the drawing must use recognizable 'conventions' to optimum effect. Models may be illustrative or analytical, again according to purpose.

ask yourself	*why* this document or drawing or model?
	for whom and to whom and from whom?
	in *what* time and place and occasion?
i.e.	*for* what purpose, with what intention, with what (precise) aim?
	or for which of several purposes seen to be related?
then	*when* should it be done and when conveyed (may be separate)
	how it should be done (less a question than an answer)
thus	why – who – what – which – when – *how*
embrace	context, relevance, completeness, sequence, tone, consistency, usage, and other things you
	may wish to consider
thus giving	*relevant form to what you do*
	from the possibilities of mode, vehicle, medium, agent, intention
	each of which can usefully be distinguished:
	they are not the same nor better described as dualities (medium: message)
NB	no statement of this kind can be value-free.
	These are the shallows of communication: hence the *apparent* case for navigation by precept.

12 Simple graphics: a strategy

Graphics is purposeful mark-making to convey messages serially
(shortening a definition by Richard Hollis). In any culture that allows of conscious form-giving within manufacture or the built environment, there will be a graphic component which will exhibit all
or some of the implicit suppositions of that culture (its 'mental
climate'). There are no essential differences of principle that distinguish graphic design from design of any other kind; merely a
respect for the purpose and the nature of the enterprise. Certain
graphic pursuits, such as typography or cartography, are most specialized studies, and to do good work in these areas does demand far
more than a sympathetic overview of their aim and attainments.
The same might be said, however, for any specialization. In nearly
all adjacent areas of design work, designers must be able to understand each other and often to work quite closely together. This will
require a superficial knowledge of the relevant discipline, and of its
special terminology, but a genuine understanding will spring from
a cultural sensibility held and exercised in common. The fact that
this is often lacking – as, for instance, by some architects in their
relations with graphic or other designers – reflects partly the divi-
sions in design education, and other factors such as the splitting-off
of so much graphic talent into the special world of high-pressure
advertising. The distinctions here are not (in other words) to be
seen as intrinsic, so much as circumstantially determined. Nor is
advertising uniquely destructive to social confidence and the possibility of decent and truthful exchanges between people; high-rise
building has recently made architects as publicly 'disreputable' as
these willing hyenas of the graphic trades.

This becomes, no doubt, an arguable matter. However, graphic
opportunities occur in simpler case: namely, in the day-to-day content of a designer's work as described in the reference section of this
book. In this respect all designers, including architects, are practising graphics for the larger part of their working lives; a fact that
is commonly overlooked. Drawings, diagrams, schedules, specifica-

tions, reports, letters – all these demand graphic decisions, which can be positive in character, or merely allowed to happen. This 'designing design' activity can have a useful effect upon the work thus served; in fact the two (the main design job, and the means for carrying it out) interpenetrate in a most interesting way. The ugly word 'communication' is helpful because it suggests an intention or desired effect (which the word 'graphics' fails to do) and because it broadens the base to include (for instance) oral questioning and model-making, neither of which involve mark-making as such. There is some confusion of terminology in all these matters. Semiotics offers a set of logical relations, and a vocabulary, that seems at first sight a useful clarification; but in practice turns out to be so dauntingly sterile and pretentious that few have the patience to grapple with it. Keeping theory to a minimum, what might be a useful strategy for beginning in graphics, and perhaps especially for architects and three-dimensional designers who need to study the subject at an elementary level?

To recapitulate, designers other than graphic specialists should see their graphic work in the simplest terms, if for nothing else as a relevantly pleasurable way of making marks on paper. They can find a practical usefulness by setting this work firmly in the full context of communication procedure in the design process. Notes on context, and criteria for evaluation, are given in part 11. Good graphic design requires an elective relation between *alphabet, image, medium,* and *process.* In a practical way, it is probably best to advance on all fronts at once:

1 Examine every graphic opportunity that normally occurs from the moment a designer accepts a commission to the ultimate filing-away of job records. Consider what has to be done to make this work enjoyable and effective.

2 Assemble a collection of useful information, including typesheets, paper samples, etc, headed by an address list and a source-list for further information when you need it, and not forgetting a key-word graphics terminology.

3   Investigate in outline the available printing processes and what is required of a layout or artwork for such purposes.

4   It is good to experiment every time you make a mark on paper, by hand or machine: why, how, when, where, what? More is learned from experiment than from perception theory, but simple logic or set theory may prove suggestive when considering the typical problems of tabular setting or organizing complex messages.

5   Consider what you have to deal with. If we read from top to bottom and from left to right, is a page or a rectangle a 'neutral' field? – and if not, what are the consequences for sequence and layout? How are units of meaning formed most effectively out of alphabet? If a paragraph is one such, think of half a dozen ways of forming a paragraph – and what is entailed. When alphabet is developed into syntax, the prime ingredients of order are *distinction, emphasis,* and *grouping,* from which a clear graphic *sequence* is derived. How might such a realization affect your attitude to scale, structure, the form of a report, the order of priorities (and their recognition) in a report? There are many considerations here and most of them can be thought through without specialized knowledge.

6   The portable typewriter was an excellent tool for ordering thought. The machine had certain in-built constraints that were a pleasure to explore: notably the 'ranged-left and open-ended' nature of the platen movement. In the desktop publishing technology that is now ubiquitous, these constraints have been replaced by what may seem infinite freedoms. Some of these freedoms are real, others can be no more than distractions. This suggests another journey of exploration: to sort out the fruitful from the useless in these computers and printers.

7   Finally, other people's work can be examined; at first hand, or, less satisfactorily, in reproduction – including of course people like Lissitzky and Max Bill who bridge across from graphics into other areas of design.

Designers who want to specialize, to become 'graphic designers' as such, will not find themselves lacking in advice or instruction from the very many schools. Such students might also wish to ask themselves just what order of reality is embraced by this work, what role-seeking and role-making is implied, how far graphic design can be a responsible trade when after all, most messages conveyed are not of the designer's choosing, and lastly, what areas of graphic design suit their own predilections and offer some experience of authenticity.

NB The suggestions in this part will find reinforcement in parts 11 ('Communication for designers'), 13 ('Drawings and models') and 16 ('Reports and report writing'). Students in schools are always obliged to document their work towards assessments and their final degree or diploma. This is a special variant on the office job-file or job-record. It is worth doing the thing properly by making an intelligible graphic sequence. The design problems are always interesting and much will be learned in the way of concise copy-writing, co-ordinates for paper sizes including folds, and consistent means of identification and retrieval. The following may be helpful as a possible check-list for such a task (for a larger job in any area of design):

1   Legend (name, job title, job number, date(s), etc.)
2   List of contents
3   Briefs (initial, and revised)
4   Note of academic situation or objectives if relevant
5   Summary of relevant job facts and other data
6   Analysis of requirements
7   Evaluation of possibilities latent in the job
8   Proposals in principle (alternatives)
9   Final proposal and reasons
10 Notes of materials, fittings, manufacture
11 Notes *re* costing
12 Report (which would normally include items 5–11 or even 1–11)
13 Action taken, modifications
14 Presentation drawings, notes, photograph of model
15 Copies of working drawings, specification, schedules

16 Machining or other instructions
17 Photographs of job process, assembly, other models, etc.
18 Photographs of final outcome
19 Test comments or user reactions generally
20 Correspondence and other job documents
21 Afterthoughts (your own criticism)
22 Job duration record (times, dates)

13 Drawings and models

It is very important to distinguish one kind of drawing or model from another – by never failing to consider its purpose, occasion, and recipient, and therefore its nature. Confusion would be avoided, and tedium minimized, if draughtsmanship were always studied in the general context of communication theory and practice; but this does not frequently happen.

Fast and skilful technical drawing as carried out in a design office is just a matter of long practice: students should not be discouraged by their first indistinct attempts. I am speaking solely of competence in technical drawing; not of satisfaction. There appear to be no short cuts to this technical facility, but common sense and a clear definition of a drawing's purpose will give a head start. Freehand drawing is something of a personal gift, valuable to a designer but not as essential to every kind of work as is usually thought – a designer can design well and not be able to draw in this way at all; conversely, a designer who draws marvellously may be mistaking his vocation as an illustrator or painter. Much design drawing – of an informal kind – is no more technically 'gifted' than mental sums transferred on to paper. Designers think and talk with sketches and diagrams, sections, full-size details; a fluent and personal use of diagrammatic technique is certainly necessary. Such work can be better seen as analytical mark-making than as analytical drawing in the classical sense. Observational drawing helps focus observation, and has all the well-attested and richer benefits from a co-ordination of hand and eye, but the transference of such gains into design procedure is an indirect one – as would be from comparable activity of other kinds.

Nothing should be taken for granted in the way of materials and instruments. The qualitative differences must be explored, compared, contrasted; if only because much of the pleasure of drawing (or modelmaking) comes from a subtle rightness in the relation of tool or instrument to material. Anyone who uses blunt tools, or confuses a Graphos pen with a clutch pencil, or who treats paper as a neutral non-material, will miss the benefit of good technique as a feedback into design thinking. These are fine-tolerance perceptions carried out at the finger tips, but awareness of them can help the tone of design responses in a very encouraging way.

Drawing practice and modelmaking will occupy a large part of a designer's time, and in a design school, even more. There will always be formal instruction in schools, but the following simple distinctions will help to place these skills in a communication context:

Diagrams are abstract, partial, energetic, concerned to establish or convey ideas and values directly, thus having an analytical or interpretive purpose. Usually have open conventions (excepting graphs and mathematical conventions), may be imprecise, or may be examining exact quantities, usually have diagnostic function.

Illustrations (including thumb-nail sketches and 'perspectives') are depictive, present appearances from which inferences may be drawn, are often atmospheric in nature and persuasive in purpose, have closed conventions. Usually have prescriptive function; better for presenting conclusions than determining them.

Surveys are records of measured and verifiable fact reduced to quantities, though survey drawings may be accompanied by interpretive notes. Closed conventions. Diagnostic function.

Working drawings are strictly purposeful and are instructions. Use rigid but propulsive conventions (i.e. lead to required action). Many types according to purpose, occasion, and recipient. Prescriptive function.

Words often have a function supplementary to drawings and models: students should note the importance of this. Many kinds of drawing and most models are too abstracted to be fully indicative of their intention. Words in this context may enquire, annotate, argue, describe, record, and otherwise supplement drawings and models, and may be written or oral or occasionally recorded on tape.

Signs, *numbers*, *codes*, etc. – clarify, regulate, supplement.

Such distinctions are helpful because they indicate the design value of the choices available – the correspondence between their form and their meaning. Once this is grasped, the whole subject ceases to be dead and conventionalized and becomes purposefully allied to other communication procedures. The worst handicap to a designer is the unintelligent way in which 'technical drawing' is sometimes taught, as a self-contained discipline quite outside any purposeful context. The point is worth repeating because some designers have to relearn technical skills and they should know that an apparent asset may turn out to be a communication liability.

The main thing is to know when a drawing can be 'free' and open in its conventions, or when it has to meet well-known and agreed conventions as are, for instance, specified in the recommendations for building drawing practice that are issued by the national bodies for standardization. As a safe general rule: always give too much information rather than too little. Drawings are no more than messages and records, they must convey fully what you intend, with no room for misunderstanding. It is a mistake to worry about the immaculate appearance of a drawing when it must be for use. In design schools, drawings become 'exhibits'. Use a notes column, on the right of the drawing.

When considering how to do a drawing, and what kind it should be, refer to the check-list at the end of part 11, and never forget to ask yourself, who will use this drawing, for what purpose, and in what context?

The distinctions of kind in drawings and models given here, are very basic: with experience, much refinement and experiment is possible, as in the development of different kinds of component and assembly drawings. This may arise either from the known context of use, or from the nature of a particular design. An example might be joinery detailing drawn out for a contractor already well-known to the designer, in which numbered components are presented – as in a cutting list for the machinist.

Models are always encouraging to work with and can be a valid form of presentation. The subject profits from a very thorough exploration of the technical possibilities, on the one band, and of the purposes involved, on the other (again, see end of part 11). Full-scale mock-ups of joint details are sometimes helpful, full-scale but drastically simplified environments are occasionally worthwhile, and of course furniture requires modelmaking at all stages, to the point where prototypes are under test. Scale models range from the quick fold-up diagram to its opposite, the doll's house illustration (see categories above) and between these extremes there is much scope for experiment.

A designer thinking out a job will go backwards and forwards from one kind of drawing or model to another, testing and exploring. Thus, as was said of communication in general, there will be a balance between subjective freedom and objective scruple; as the job develops 'the chosen means become precise'.

14   Survey before plan

As when Le Corbusier says that 'architecture is organization', the notion of survey is shorthand rhetoric; implying that very much more is connoted or at least hinted at, than the simple requirement of a clear and adequate drawing – of what? – the ground plan? What is implied, centrally, is the significance of the plan (both the intention, the forecast, and the horizontal section) and of its *grounded and verifiable base* in number (reduction to quantities) and fact (as distinct from opinion or judgement). Another banner unfurls: 'the plan is the generator'. Thus the notion of 'survey' acquires, if not mystical overtones, then certainly a special weight of responsibility. If realism is the watchword, don't con yourself or anyone else; get the facts right and get all the facts. Test every step forward. The attraction of such polemic is almost a measure of its essential fallibility. Even at the simplest executive level, that of measurement and record, for which prior status is claimed by the seeming neutrality of the procedures, we know that human beings are impossibly inventive, both in the selectivity of their vision, and the wild unreliability of their memories. With respect to their deeper fallibility, we are now as chary of Five Year Plans as of planners in general, with their sometimes compulsive itch for tidiness at the cost of spontaneity; yet the notion of survey, of finding out what you can *first* and as accurately as you can, is still intactly a reasonable undertaking wherever quantities are in question.

The notes that follow are an aid to so doing, at the simple level of a space or a building that requires to be measured; free of all cosmic misgiving as to what might be done with it. Readers must form their own weighting of such implicitness. Designers will be aware that a surveyor is a specialist, one upon whose services a designer may have to lean occasionally, and it should be clear that these introductory notes do not approach this level of expertise, nor do they involve equipment for which special tuition is necessary. Even so it is surprising how the simplest job (say, measuring up a room or a flat or a small shop with a view to conversion or fitting out) can go wrong, prove to be wrongly or insufficiently observed and recorded.

The context of such a task goes in with the designer in two respects. First, in a literal way the surrounding context of any such small volume will need to be looked into, analysed, and in certain ways questioned and recorded. Second, the character of the spaces involved will not only commend themselves (as having certain features, relations, categories) but if at this stage the job itself is known, or is known to be 'one of a kind' already familiar to the designer, it is inevitable that matching will begin to take place. This matching will tend to produce 'fit' between known categories of use or function in the job, or categories that are typical of it, to differentiation within the spaces that are being surveyed. In other words, ideas jump the gun and begin to form around the special formal attributes that begin to be revealed. This occurs as the structural logic of a building begins to unfold, so that 'surfaces' begin to have distinctive character instead of being undifferentiated (for example, as between the outward expression of a load-bearing wall built of brick, and that of a partition wall built of plaster and laths on studding). Gradually the essential structure and volume stand revealed together with accessory situations that may well be swept away or modified.

These matters are not easy to describe, the real point here is that these survey procedures (like asking questions, writing reports, etc.) are *already design* and should be approached in that spirit. A survey should never be treated as a technical exercise. The imagination should be at work discovering such spatial possibilities as seem inherently available, and matching them with imagined uses. This is valid and natural (not 'formalist') because the designer will include within his ordinary competence an adequate testing of every hypothesis he forms, upon the test-bed of 'requiredness' (a Gestalt term) in the job as this in turn begins to assume a structure. The inherent logical relations of the one (the building) must work for those of the other (the job, or 'the problem' or 'the opportunities revealed'). For these reasons attitude of mind is very important in survey work (as in diagnostic procedures generally). Alertness is a state of mind that can be summoned and sustained by an act of will. A new situation must be entered watchfully, but also with a certain leniency of predisposition, a willingness to be engaged (to enter into transactional parlance). As when asking questions a designer must learn how to listen, so he must learn to absorb impressions in survey work; a building must be felt for. Given experience, technique, and a productive attitude that always has an ingredient of respect, a building or spatial situation will be found to speak for itself. Not, however, if a designer has never learned to listen. Although most remarks in this part (and all those that follow) are about building surveys, there is a general sense in which any situation of 'survey' will yield responsively to the right balance of sympathy and disciplined enquiry, of which careful measurement and drawing are merely component experiences. It follows of course that if a designer wishes to exclude personal response from a survey, it is better to have the job done by a professions surveyor (or colleague).

Getting down to brass tacks, and taking the simple building survey as the typical case for the rest of this part, the notes begin with some guiding considerations, and there follows a check-list that should be of practical help.

1   Do your homework first by gathering preliminary information including district maps.

2   Make sure you have a full kit of instruments as described in the check-list; if not, go back for anything missing *before* making a start.

3   Be prepared to note everything down; but *everything*. The commonest mistake by beginners is trusting to memory. It is more realistic to suppose that nothing exists of which you have no record.

4   Use overlays to separate out different kinds of information (formed simply by using thin detail or tracing paper) and have two underlay grids to help freehand drawing (squared and iso- or axonometric). See check-list. It is essential to have a mounting board, with clip, so that sheets of notes are under control rather than on a dusty floor. Supplement all measurement with the camera and sketching.

5   Enter old buildings alertly, on the prowl for trouble. Note any evidence of smell, subsidence, cracking, rot, woodworm, damp, loose plaster, stuck doors, pattern staining, damaged fittings.

6   Note subjective impressions immediately (actually note them on paper).

7   Number, write, and draw clearly, even if it seems slow; if not you will always regret it (and end up wasting more time).

8   The same applies to the thoroughness with which you take and note measurements. It wastes much more time to rush the job and to be obliged to come back (perhaps more than once) for missing information.

9   Always note the superficial nature and conditions of surfaces, but

10   Always go beyond surfaces, to structure, and to an awareness of materials. When you have to make intelligent guesses, say so.

11   Always note and differentiate load-bearing walls from (potentially movable) partition walls and from party walls (common to adjacent premises) and measure apertures in their true structural sizes (linings can be noted separately).

12   A careful record of joist intervals is essential, future load-bearing decisions may depend on it. Also ceiling rafters, studding, and any other concealed relevant information that could affect fixtures and fittings.

13   Measure from one point, line, or surface, or errors will be cumulative. Work off struck chalk datum lines, off which measurements can be triangulated at regular intervals. Always use diagonals, and plenty of them.

14   Make full-size drawings of mouldings, architraves, etc, using when necessary a pin moulding template.

15   Note vertical heights that may be worth respecting (apart from those noted as a matter of course).

16   Estimate and carefully note all relevant information to extend the space you are concerned with into its immediate environment. This will include, obviously, 'the neighbours', but also physical situations like drainage, structural matters, facade or elevational relationships, light, views, aspect, and a service analysis to include waste disposal, plumbing, electricity, deliveries, etc. (see check-list).

17   Note any matters of possible concern to by-laws and local authorities (this needs experience).

18   Note all socket outlets, plumbing, etc, but do not waste time carefully drawing up superficial fittings that are obviously expendable.

Survey check-list
excluding special instruments

take
Container (purpose-made)
Carrier board with clip, hardboard or ply, size to suit
     (min. 25 x 40 cm)
Paper, detail and/or tracing
Grid underlays
Pencils and pens, include colours
Eraser
Penknife and/or small pencil sharpener
Chalk and lines
Drawing pins and lead weights
Sticky tape
Plumbline
Pocket rule-tape (imperial and metric), 3 metres
Rule-tape not less than 10 metres
Folding boxwood rule, 2 metres, for verticals

Pocket compass
Spirit level
Water levels if required
Angle bevel and protractor
Pin moulding template
Short metal rule (for carrier board)
Torch, batteries checked
Probe or birdcage awl
Camera with spare film and flash
Hammer (light)
Tape-recorder if relevant
Maps, drawings, case notes, keys, relevant phone numbers
Small stoppered container for specimens

NB the above will fit into a very small container made for the job;
survey can be done (and often is) with less than this elementary
equipment, but there are sensible reasons for all inclusions

check
Area notes by map and observation
Street access, width, pavements, planting, drainage
Traffic flow, direction, feeder sources, volume
Traffic parking (question for after working hours)
Bus services and stops (and underground train if relevant)
Train services and station access
Noise
Litter
Street aspect by compass
Relevant heights and light cut-off
Stop-cocks and other control points for services
Waste collection arrangements
Delivery arrangements
Telephone
Line TV and aerials
Water, gas and electricity supplies
Drainage
Gardens and planting
Facilities: doctor, hospital, library, laundry, pub, stores

Milk deliveries
Garaging
Pram or wheeled access
Adjoining buildings
Other possible interests
Roof condition and structures (as estimated without ladders)
Exterior wall condition
Pointing, gables, barge-boards, soffits, trim, footings, steps, paths
Exterior doors and windows
Locks
Provisions for post and deliveries
Bells, handles, porches, mats
Security measures

First impressions of interior and entry
Hall or reception area
Stairs
Lifts
Sound
Light
Smell
Temperature
Humidity
Maintenance
Surfaces, paintwork, paper, plaster, etc.
Structure
Materials
Circulation
Doors
Skirting
Floors and floorboards (widths, direction, material, pattern)
Joists, trimmers
Hearths
Fireplaces
Vents
Windows
Ceilings
Rafters

Mouldings
Built-in cupboards
Light
Aspect
Views
Electricity gas and water switches, taps, outlets, etc.
Telephone and TV
Metering for services
Heating systems
Insulation
Washing and bathing facilities
Kitchen and serving facilities
Cleaning facilities
WC facilities
Attic access
Roof structure and condition
Tanks and other services
Guttering and downpipes

NB estimate age and condition wherever relevant in a survey (and note)

15   Asking questions

The notes are confined to enquiry in the particulars of design practice. More general and more searching questions are professionally
relevant – to fail to ask them is to invite creative anaemia – but
such questioning is ill-served by precept. Though perhaps it helps to
jump over molehills before climbing mountains.

Most design problems will be presented in ways that may be
diffuse, ill-defined, or actually misleading; yet, a problem cannot be
resolved in any satisfactory sense before its nature has been determined. According to the 'problem', such discovery may be instanta-
neous, or the problem itself simply invented by the designer in an
extremely open situation; in either of these cases it is unhelpful
to use the word, or to conceive of design as problem-solving: a different order of resourcefulness will be required. However, keeping
to the work which has been used as an illustration, the designer
will be asking himself and others a continuous stream of questions,
some of which may need to be formally stated or written down. The
reasons for this:

1   To gain an awareness of the problem that is sufficiently objective, i.e. takes full account of relevant facts, relevant interests, relevant possibilities, relevant limitations.

2   To focus and clarify your own response to the job and to exclude
(as far as possible) irrelevant responses – those that might belong to
different jobs still strong in memory, that might be a simple projec-
tion of your own interests, or that might prejudge certain issues
before you have investigated them.

3   To enable you to sense out the feel, weight, context of the job
and relate yourself productively to its potential (to turn yourself
toward it).

4   To enable you to construct a satisfactory working brief, i.e. clear and agreed terms of reference.

General considerations:

1   The extent to which formal questioning is necessary will vary from job to job, but has nothing to do with the *apparent* scale or simplicity of the problem you encounter – questioning may extend or alter the possibilities beyond recognition.

2   It should be recognized that diagnostic work has a creative component, a kind of dialogue between you and the client or between you and the total situation you are examining; thus its instrumental success very much depends on your own attitude and approach. To ask the right questions is not to carry out a tiresome preliminary to design; it is already design, and it may require considerable imaginative effort on your part. In the answer to one question is the genesis of the next.

3   Questions served up 'cold' will harvest facts, but may leave untouched all manner of subjective or non-measurable factors which may be crucial to the understanding of a problem. Most (not all) problems will involve a client; most will involve human relationships, and therefore tact and an effort of identification with other people's viewpoints.

4   Your intention in asking questions must be reflected both in their structure and in their tone; categories of question useful to you may not be useful to the client or invoke helpful associations in his mind only later, as abstract categories assume concrete reference, will you be talking on convergent terms with your client.

5   (Tone: 'the speaker ... chooses or arranges his words differently as his audience varies, in automatic or deliberate recognition of his relation to them. The tone of his utterance reflects his awareness of this relation, his sense of how he stands towards those he is addressing' – I. A. Richards). A suitable tone does not always imply informality, or prevent you from arranging your questions into cat-

egories, but may well require a careful choice of terms in describing them or introducing them.

6   The designer is acting as an agent in a process which (viewed in retrospect) may appear to have discovered itself over an extended period of time; questioning takes place across the flux of decision-making in a variety of situations. Early on, personal observation will involve self-questioning.

7   There is often value in mixing questions by free association; but concealed or subsequent categorizing will in itself provide association, and categories relevant to questions will usually be relevant to the answers.

8   Many questions are best put in a form that suggests typical answers, or alternatively put as assumptions that can be agreed with or corrected. Such assumptions need framing with some care, or you may cut out their possible suggestiveness and thus 'short circuit' back to where you started. Stated assumptions work best at the extremes either as a mild confirmation of something fairly obvious, or as something so outrageous that a lively response is inevitable.

9   It is a mistake to rely on formal means to establish informal truths. Facts are best investigated formally; opinions or attitudes informally. A client may shy away from an attitude imputed to him by the way you have put a question in writing, whereas face-to-face things would have been different.

10   In formulating written questions, remember it is difficult for someone to withdraw a direct answer to which he has committed himself, unless you can show reason that he was misinformed. Commitment may be useful on matters of fact, but on matters of opinion may merely express prejudice. Taking this further, if you are working with someone toward some common end, you must allow their prejudice as much breathing space as your own; but don't carelessly drive them into positions from which they can't retract without loss of face, and which may come to impinge on your common activity quite needlessly.

11   Of course facts and opinions will be inextricably mixed in your client's experience of his problem; hence the delicacy of your diagnostic technique.

12   As a rider to that, be careful not to confuse diagnosis with cure. Questions seek answers; not a euphoria of perpetual doubt.

13   Loosely and vaguely-put written questions are quite useless. A 'portmanteau' question will receive a portmanteau answer, and also diminish your client's confidence ('what is he getting at?'). Questions are best put singly and profusely – unless you have a particular purpose in mind.

14   Consider carefully when and when not to use tapes, cameras, and notebooks. The contextual requirement (in the design sequence, see part 10) must be balanced against consideration of tact and judgement.

15   Questions and answers qualify and reinforce – *but do not substitute* – judgement and decision.

Oral questioning at informal meetings:

1   Above all, remember that to question is not to interrogate.

2   Mental alertness is essential (not so obvious).

3   Leading questions may be fruitful as guides to intention or attitude in those present; questions can be put in this way at such meetings that could not be asked in more formal circumstances (or in writing).

4   Do not take your answers too literally – unless they refer to matters of fact (which can always be checked) it is necessary to take conversational answers or assertions at less than their face value.

5   It is difficult to establish needs by direct questioning, but relatively easy to establish desires, preferences, prejudice, and opinion based on specific experiences. Motivation is far more elusive.

6   Do not allow the nature or sequence of questions to get on to 'tramlines' – closed patterns of thinking – which may give you a false run of evidence.

7   Avoid giving an impression (which should anyway be unwarranted) that you have made up your mind and are merely asking questions as a matter of form.

8   Make some allowance for positive and negative appearing in a misleading juxtaposition: e.g. if challenged, a person with authoritarian habits may stress his anti-authoritarian ideas or desires. Most people have inbuilt compensations for exaggerated personality traits and they are delighted to be able to exercise them.

9   It is off-putting to ask questions conversationally from your notebook.

10   A useful extension of questioning technique is the meeting at which all parties concerned air their views at random, with you keeping the thing going as a sort of group therapist. The purpose of such a meeting should be understood by all concerned. Avoid the meeting becoming a collective instructional session leaving no subsequent room for manoeuvre. Such meetings can be time-savers, particularly where many people are involved, but they should be followed up by more scrupulous enquiry, whether or not such enquiry starts from inferences drawn from the meeting.

NB   In all this the designer is meeting a situation, not attempting to master it. The only value of conscious technique here is in making the designer more useful, because more accurately responsive, to the situation he is serving, and perhaps a bit less liable to take his own unquestioning assumptions for granted.

Reminder:
During the diagnostic phase of design work you will (with respect to what confronts you and what you have to seek out) observe, compare, relate, distinguish, question, discuss, 'research', measure, estimate, and record. This might be said to be your diagnostic shopping list.

When considering, the constraints in a job (constraints: 'a re-stricting condition' [Chambers Dictionary], factors that impinge up-on a job, that must be taken into account, that belong to its terms of reference but may he unstated as such) – remember two things. First, a necessary distinction between constants and variables, and second, that you must search for *agreement, conflict, latitude,* and *determination* within your constraint system.

Finally, it is quite proper to redefine your intention and ob-jectives in the light of a constraint and opportunity analysis, and from there to establish the principles that seem necessary to respect both; but a design *concept* cannot be 'defined' as an embodiment of principles; it merely has a structure of required argument to be offered against. Otherwise design would indeed be very easy.

The constraints on which students are usually (and understand-ably) weak, are the budget, restrictions in law, the allowable time for design work in its various aspects, and design predilections and/ or experience (which will slant an individual designer's approach, however 'objective' he tries to be). It is necessary to know that such factors may be weightily influential in design decisions.

16   Reports and report writing

A report is a written statement of fact and opinion, addressed to clients or to colleagues (or to oneself). A report may be retrospective, and therefore a terminal objective in some series of happenings, but usually its purpose is seen as a more active one: to support, explain, or gain agreement to a suggested course of action.

Designers have good reasons for employing the report as a familiar and often indispensable communication vehicle. Used properly, a report will more than repay the labour of its preparation. A report can describe, interpret, and analyse a situation with sensitivity and suggestiveness, and in language that any ordinary person will understand. For clients, or indeed anyone else whose interests must be consulted, there are no difficulties of transposition (as from drawings to words) that might inhibit a full preliminary discussion. There might of course be transpositive problems of style, if the report has been badly done (failing to respect its purpose and recipient). In the early stages of a job, a client may be wary of a designer's drawings, however seductively presented: the medium is not his own, and may conceal all manner of implied decisions which he can only take on trust. Sometimes the client will discharge his unease by demanding entirely unnecessary alterations, or he may even reject the first design out of hand, until he has been reassured by a set of drawn-out alternatives. This is a very hit-and-miss way of going on. A preliminary report gives confidence, because here is evidence that the problems have been examined with professional thoroughness. There is also the possibility of active intervention on his part *before* the design reaches the drawing board. A client who enjoys a real sense of participation in all the thinking that surrounds the design process may be ready to accept a radical and (for him) unfamiliar design solution, simply because he has understood the genesis of the solution in the problem itself. Thus may a very conservative client find himself embarking upon inconceivable adventures, and enjoying them.

These are obvious benefits to a designer's work, but reports can do far more than this primitive midwifery. In work of complex nature, reports may have the key role of a more subtle, creative, and constituent process. The writing of a report will order (and externalize) a designer's own thinking, and will enable him to call in question his own working assumptions – before it is too late. The designer will not only avoid misunderstandings with his client – a negative gain – but may also attain a new understanding of the task, both from the discussion that such a report will inevitably precipitate, and from the effort involved in arguing out a problem analysis. Normally a report is neither a brief nor an analysis as such, but rather a distillation from analytical thinking; expressed in terms which will farther a diagnosis into relevant action. A brief must always be redefined when feasibility studies are complete, or when the problem can be freshly seen after due thought and examination by the designer. A report may include a suggested redefinition, or may merely point to its necessity. Finally, it must be realized that a large-scale job is a co-operative venture. It is a courtesy to give all concerned a document that makes plain the reasons for a design and their own part in it (this applies to design colleagues and consultants, but also to contractors).

It is sometimes said that all this is far better done over a glass of sherry at the club (designers are assumed to feel at home in all possible worlds) or perhaps during the main course of one of those interminable businessmen's lunches. In practice, a designer will have any number of informal meetings with his clients, at any one of which the burden of a report may be freely discussed. A report is a formal document that can be taken home and considered at leisure, or may be passed for comment to business associates, and to others whose interests may be involved. A report is also, indubitably, a record (though not a legally binding one). Reports have their own usefulness – they are not a substitute for conversations, contracts, letters, questionnaires, drawings, or other vehicles of communication.

Reports should be reasonably concise and readable (obviously), but beginners sometimes forget that style (meaning here, tone of voice) is equally important. Those who lack experience of writing should use short words and short sentences, making quite sure that the structure of the report has within it a clear and logical sequence.

More confident writers will tend to adjust the tone of their writing to their purpose and to their awareness of the reader. At all costs avoid bombast, rhetoric, excessive technicality, and those knowing turns of phrase that imply ignorance on the part of the reader. A report so written may have unfortunate consequences.

The following notes summarize the active functions of a report, and the more obvious factors that should be kept in mind. There are less stringent requirements for the kind of report that merely supplements a set of detailed proposals (e.g. presentation drawings).

Reports:

1 must be written in full awareness of their purpose and occasion and the receiver (the nature, purpose, and occasion of a report should always be stated at the beginning, however informally)

2 require an imaginative awareness of the person(s) addressed, and thus an appropriate *tone* of address

3 should communicate in a direct, sequential, and consistent manner (derived from 1 and 2)

4 have no 'correct' structure, merely an appropriate one

5 will generally follow the logical sequence of given–required–proposed, though not necessarily a formal structure

6 should normally keep clear of design jargon and private language, using the word 'I' with discretion

7 should argue syntactically, adding questions or known facts or quantities in tabular form (preferably separated as a supplement to the report)

8 may include sketches, diagrams, graphs, photographs, etc, either as a supplement or directly related to the text

9 if lengthy, should use short paragraphs which can be numbered to facilitate reference back

10 if lengthy, should also begin with a summary of conclusions but not, desirably, a summary of recommendations as such (better to let the argument require them)

11 may be read (and handled) by several people; to advantage, several (numbered) copies may be offered

12 must be complete and self-explanatory (the writer may not be present to make good any omissions)

13 should provide a professional interpretation of the problem that concerns your client

14 should thus establish for the client the full implications of the brief he has given the designer

15 should relate such implications to the 'constraints' in the problem (e.g. time, money, space, legal restrictions, etc, etc.)

16 should thus provide both an insight into the client's needs and the intentions behind the brief, and an estimate of the true possibilities latent in the brief

17 should thus clarify for designer and client the margin of free choice available

18 should certainly make clear the context of present decisions or recommended action

19 unless concerned with specific decisions, will be concerned to adduce relevant principles which such action must respect

20 most important of all, should gain a sense of priority both in the needs and potential of a situation

21 should seek a client's agreement to a designer's working assumptions, and any foreseeable issue of principle that may bias the design approach

22 should recommend and define subsequent action (how, when, what)

23 may anticipate (require, provide for) a positive response from the client or persons addressed

24 may lead to a fresh and more explicit definition of the design brief

25 should be a creative task in the design process (constituent, not accessory)

26 should thus be directly helpful to the designer, and may even in some cases be written to himself or to colleagues concerned with the job

27 should be regarded as a design opportunity – construction, layout, materials, should not be overworked in relation to the content of the report, but should look and feel right in terms of 1–4

In summary, it may be said that report writing has three special merits: the conventions are as open as the use of the language in which they are written, and can be shaped accordingly (to a close match of form and purpose); a report is a prompt to active participation by all concerned, and is thus both a catalyst and a vehicle of consultation, and a report can function with salutary effect at different stages of the design process – notably, those of analysis and presentation (see parts 10 and 11). A report can also, of course, provide conclusions, and can thus be (for a consultant's purpose) the required end-result of his assignment. For some designers – by no means all – report writing can be a good way of 'talking out' a job, or considerations that surround it, in a way that is more reflective and logically sequential than ordinary talk, and less transitory. For all these reasons, here is a skill worth learning – necessarily, by arduous practice. Designers for whom writing is not congenial, can use the report device at its leanest and most purposeful: as a tabular listing of relevant notes that simply accompany drawings and/or models; or as tabular notes that accompany spoken presentation of proposals. (Tabular: like a shopping list.) The check-list at the end of part 11 should be helpful in writing reports of any kind.

The list comprises most titles mentioned in this book: it should be consulted in conjunction with 'Reading for design' (part 7). As will be clear from that discussion, this list (which was made first in 1980) does not offer a full and balanced recommendation for design reading; it is also too long for that purpose. Students will and should find their own priorities. Nevertheless, the list will have its uses. Details of the first British edition are generally given; place of publication is London, unless otherwise indicated. Many of these titles will also be available, from time to time, in reprinted editions.

Abercrombie, M.L.J, *The anatomy of judgement*, Hutchinson, 1960

Alexander, Christopher, *Notes on the synthesis of form*, Cambridge Mass: Harvard University Press, 1964

— *The timeless way building*, New York: Oxford University Press, 1979

Anarchy (magazine), ed. Colin Ward, 1961–70

Archer, L.Bruce, *Systematic method for designers*, Council of Industrial Design, 1965

Ashbee, C.R, *Craftsmanship in competitive industry*, Campden: Essex House Press, 1908

— *Should we stop teaching art?* Batsford, 1911

Association for Planning and Regional Reconstruction, *Survey before plan* (series), Lund Humphries, [1945]

Aylward, Bernard, *Design education in schools*, Evans, 1973

Ballantine, Richard, *Richard's bicycle book*, Pan Books, 1975

Bauhaus Books, nos. 1–14, Munich: Albert Langen, 1925–30. (Facsimiles and new editions, Mainz/Berlin: Florian Kupferberg, 1965–; some English editions, Lund Humphries)

Bayer, Herbert, and Walter Gropius, Ise Gropius (ed.), *Bauhaus 1919–1928*, New York: Museum of Modern Art, 1938

Beazley, Elisabeth, *Design and detail of the space between buildings*, Architectural Press, 1960

Benedict, Ruth, *Patterns of culture*, Routledge & Kegan Paul, 1935

Benton, Tim, and Charlotte Benton, with Dennis Sharp (ed.), *Form and function*, Crosby Lockwood Staples, 1975

Berneri, M.L, *Journey through Utopia*, Routledge & Kegan Paul, 1950

Boardman, Philip, *The worlds of Patrick Geddes*, Routledge & Kegan Paul, 1978

Buber, Martin, *Between man and man*, Routledge & Kegan Paul, 1947

— *The way of man*, Routledge & Kegan Paul, 1950

— *Paths in Utopia*, Boston: Beacon Press, 1958

Cantacuzino, Sherban, *Wells Coates*, Gordon Fraser, 1978

Capell, Richard, *Schubert's songs*, 3rd edn, Pan Books, 1973

Cooley, Mike, *Architect or bee? the human price of technology*, 2nd edn, Hogarth Press, 1987

Cox, C.B, and A.E.Dyson, Rhodes Boyson (ed.), *Black papers on education*, nos. 1–5, 1969–77

Crawford, Alan, *C.R.Ashbee*, New Haven: Yale University Press, 1985

Creswell, H.B, *The Honeywood file*, Architectural Press, 1929

Cross, Nigel, David Elliott and Robin Roy (ed.), *Man-made futures*, Hutchinson, 1974

Cullen, Gordon, *The concise townscape*, Architectural Press, 1971

Curtis, William J.R, *Modern architecture since 1900* (1982), 3rd edn, Phaidon, 1996

Davie, Donald, *Articulate energy: an enquiry into the syntax of English poetry*, Routledge & Kegan Paul, 1955

Domus Books (Quaderni di Domus), ed. Lina Bo & Carlo Pagani, Milan: Editoriale Domus, 1945–

Duberman, Martin, *Black Mountain: an exploration in community*, Wildwood House, 1974

Eagleton, Terry, *Literary theory*, Oxford: Blackwell, 1983

Ecologist, The (editors of), *A blueprint for survival*, Harmondsworth: Penguin Books, 1972

Form (magazine), Cambridge, 1966–9

Finch, Janet and Michael Rustin (ed.), *A degree of choice: higher education: a right to learn*, Harmondsworth: Penguin Books, 1986

Frampton, Kenneth, *Modern architecture: a critical history* (1980), 3rd edn, Thames & Hudson, 1992

Fromm, Erich, *Fear of freedom*, Routledge & Kegan Paul, 1942
— *The sane society*, Routledge & Kegan Paul, 1956

Froshaug, Anthony, *Typographic norms*, Birmingham: Kynoch Press (with Design & Art Directors Association, London), 1964

Gabo, Naum, and J. L. Martin, Ben Nicholson (ed.), *Circle*, Faber & Faber, 1937

Ghyka, Matila, *A practical handbook of geometrical composition and design*, Tiranti, 1956

Giedion, Sigfried, *Space, time and architecture* (1941), 5th edn, Cambridge Mass: Harvard University Press, 1967
— *Mechanization takes command*, New York: Oxford University Press, 1948
— *The eternal present* trilogy (New York: Oxford University Press): *The beginnings of art* (1962), *The beginnings of architecture* (1964), *Architecture and the phenomena of transition* (Cambridge Mass: Harvard University Press, 1971)

Goffman, Erving, *Encounters*, Indianapolis: Bobbs Merrill, 1961
— *Interaction ritual*, Chicago: Aldine, 1967
(and other books)

Goodman, Paul, *Compulsory miseducation*, Harmondsworth: Penguin Books, 1971

Goodman, Percival, and Paul Goodman, *Communitas*, Chicago: Chicago University Press, 1947

Goslett, Dorothy, *The professional practice of design*, 2nd edn, Batsford, 1978

Green, Ronald, *The architect's guide to running a job*, 3rd edn, Architectural Press, 1972

Gropius, Walter, *The new architecture and the Bauhaus*, Faber & Faber, 1935

Guinness Oswald, *The dust of death*, Leicester: Inter-Varsity, 1973

Hayward, Charles, *Woodworker's pocket book*, Evans, 1971

Hornsey College of Art (students and staff), *The Hornsey affair*, Harmondsworth: Penguin Books, 1969

Illich, Ivan D, *Deschooling society*, Harmondsworth: Penguin Books, 1971

Jencks, Charles, *The language of post-modern architecture*, 2nd edn, Academy Editions, 1978
— and George Baird (ed.), *Meaning in architecture*, Barrie & Rockliffe, 1969
Jones, J. Christopher, *Design methods*, Chichester: Wiley, 1970

King, Anthony D. (ed.), *Buildings and society*, Routledge & Kegan Paul, 1980
Kitchen, Paddy, *A most unsettling person: an introduction to the ideas and life of Patrick Geddes*, Gollancz, 1975
Koestler, Arthur, *The act of creation*, Hutchinson, 1964
Koffka, Kurt, *Principles of Gestalt psychology*, Routledge & Kegan Paul, 1935
Köhler, Wolfgang, *Gestalt psychology*, Bell, 1930
— *The place of value in a world of facts*, Routledge & Kegan Paul, 1939
Kron, Joan, and Suzanne Slesin, *High-tech*, Allen Lane, 1979
Kropotkin, Peter, *Fields, factories and workshops*, Hutchinson, 1899. (Edited and with new material by Colin Ward: *Fields, factories and workshops tomorrow*, George Allen & Unwin, 1974)
— *Mutual aid: a factor of evolution*, Heinemann, 1902

Le Corbusier, *Towards a new architecture*, John Rodker, 1927. (Facsimile edition, Architectural Press, 1970)
— *Oeuvre complète* (ed. W. Boesiger), Zurich: Girsberger, 1929–
Lethaby, W. R, *Form in civilization* (1922), 2nd edn, Oxford University Press, 1957
— aphorisms, see Roberts (below)
Lissitzky-Küppers, Sophie, *El Lissitsky: life, letters, texts*, Thames & Hudson, 1968
Logie, Gordon, *Furniture from machines*, George Allen & Unwin, 1948

MacEwan, Malcolm, *Crisis in architecture*, RIBA Publications, 1974
Martin, Bruce, *Standards and building*, RIBA Publications, 1971
— *Joints in buildings*, George Godwin, 1977

Martin, J.L, and S.Speight, *The flat book*, Heinemann, 1939

Matrix, *Making space: women and the man-made environment*, Pluto Press, 1984

Medawar, Peter, *The art of the soluble*, Methuen, 1967

— *Induction and intuition in scientific thought*, Methuen, 1969

Mitchell, Percy, *A boatbuilder's story*, St Austell: Kingston Publications, 1968

Moholy-Nagy, Laszló, *The new vision*, 3rd edn, New York: Wittenborn, 1946

Mumford, Lewis, *Technics and civilization*, Routledge & Kegan Paul, 1934

— *The culture of cities*, Secker & Warburg, 1938

— *The condition of man*, Secker & Warburg, 1944

Nairn, Tom, and Angelo Quattrocchi, *The beginning of the end*, Panther Books, 1968

Needham, Joseph, *Science and civilisation in China*, Cambridge: Cambridge University Press, 1954–

Neill, A.S, *Summerhill: a radical approach to education*, Gollancz, 1962

Open University, *History of architecture and design 1890–1939* (A305: course units), Milton Keynes: Open University Press, 1975

— *Man-made futures: design and technology* (T262: course units), Milton Keynes: Open University Press, 1975

Papanek, Victor, *Design for the real world*, Thames & Hudson, 1972

Pateman, Trevor (ed.), *Counter course: a handbook for course criticism*, Harmondsworth: Penguin Books, 1972

Peters, R.S, *Ethics and education*, George Allen & Unwin, 1966 (and other books)

Pevsner, Nikolaus, *Pioneers of modern design*, 3rd edn, Harmondsworth: Penguin Books, 1960

Pirsig, Robert M, *Zen and the art of motor cycle maintenance*, Bodley Head, 1974

Pound, Ezra, *ABC of reading*, Faber & Faber, 1951

Pye, David, *The nature and art of workmanship*, Cambridge: Cambridge University Press, 1968

Rasch, Heinz, and Bodo Rasch, *Der Stuhl*, Stuttgart: Akademischer
    Verlag Fritz Wedekind, 1928
Read, Herbert, *Art and industry* (1934), 4th edn, Faber & Faber, 1956
— *Anarchy and order*, Faber & Faber, 1945
— *Education through art* (1943), revised edn, Faber & Faber, 1958
Rée, Harry, *Educator extraordinary: the life and achievement of Henry
    Morris 1889–1961*, Longman, 1973
Reich, Wilhelm, *The function of the orgasm*, Panther Books, 1968
Reimer, Everett, *School is dead: an essay on alternatives*, Harmonds-
    worth: Penguin Books, 1971
*Report from the Select Committee on Education and Science: session
    1968–69: student relations* (7 vols.), HMSO, 1969
Richards, I. A, *Practical criticism*, Routledge & Kegan Paul, 1929
Roberts, A. R. N, *William Richard Lethaby 1857–1931*, LCC Central
    School of Arts & Crafts, 1957
Roszak, Theodore, *The making of a counter-culture*, Faber & Faber,
    1970
Roth, Alfred (ed.), *The new architecture*, Zurich: Les Éditions
    d'Architecture, 1940
Rubens, Godfrey, *William Richard Lethaby*, Architectural Press, 1986

Salaman, R. A, *Dictionary of tools, used in the woodworking and allied
    trades, c. 1700–1970*, George Allen & Unwin, 1975
Samson, Frederic, *Dotes and antidotes*, Royal College of Art, 1979
Schumacher, E. F, *Small is beautiful*, Blond & Briggs, 1973
— *A guide for the perplexed*, Blond & Briggs, 1977
— *Good work*, Jonathan Cape, 1979
Sharp, Dennis (ed.), *Planning and architecture: essays presented to
    Arthur Korn by the Architectural Association*, Barrie & Rockliff,
    1967
— (ed.) *The rationalists*, Architectural Press, 1978
Skelton, Robin (ed.), *Herbert Read: a memorial symposium*, Methuen,
    1970
Smithson, Peter, *Bath: walks within walls*, Bath: Adams & Dart, 1971
Sommer, Robert, *Tight spaces: hard architecture and how to human-
    ize it*, Englewood Cliffs: Prentice-Hall, 1974
Spencer, Herbert, *Pioneers of modern typography*, Lund Humphries,
    1969

Steiner, George, *Language and silence*, Faber & Faber, 1967

Sturt, George, *The wheelwright's shop*, Cambridge: Cambridge University Press, 1923

Thompson, E. P, *William Morris: romantic to revolutionary* (1955), revised edn, Merlin Press, 1977

Toffler, Alvin, *Future shock*, Bodley Head, 1970

Tschichold, Jan, *Typographische Gestaltung*, Basel: Benno Schwabe, 1935. (English edition: *Asymmetric typography*, Faber & Faber, 1967)

Turner, John F. C, *Housing by people*, Marion Boyars, 1976

Ulm (magazine), Ulm: Hochschule für Gestaltung, 1958–68

Wachsmann, Konrad, *The turning point of building*, New York: Van Nostrand Reinhold, 1961

Ward, Colin, *The child in the city*, Architectural Press, 1978

— (ed.) *Vandalism*, Architectural Press, 1973

Watkin, David, *Morality and architecture*, Oxford: Oxford University Press, 1977

Whitehead, A. N, *The aims of education*, Williams & Norgate, 1929

Whole Earth Catalog, *The last Whole Earth Catalog*, Harmondsworth: Penguin Books, 1971

— *Whole Earth epilog*, Harmondsworth: Penguin Books, 1974

Whyte, L. L. (ed.), *Aspects of form* (1951), 2nd edn, Lund Humphries, 1968

Wingler, Hans M, *The Bauhaus*, Cambridge Mass: MIT Press, 1969

Woodcock, George, *Herbert Read: the stream and the source*, Faber & Faber, 1972

Wooden Boat (magazine), Manchester NH, USA

Zevi, Bruno, *The modern language of architecture*, Washington: University of Washington Press, 1978

18   Advice for beginners

1   Question every brief and *rewrite* it to be sufficiently clear, full, and definite. If you must make certain assumptions of your own, state them. Get agreement for your final version. Then proceed. Fail to do this and you will fail in understanding design.

2   Attitude: if you climb on top of a job, trying to master it, the work will suffocate. *Let it take you, play with it, search for its own life.*

3   Don't be conned into thinking that only new materials or processes are worth investigating. Every material available is strictly contemporary.

4   Out of every job that seems an indistinct mess, try to rescue one small part that is clear, simple, definite, and very well made or done.

5   In many studio projects there is an academic reality – work for you and your tutor – and an 'as-if' reality – work on the job itself. Should you separate them? How?

6   If you are miserably dissatisfied with your work on a job, make your answer to it a detailed self-criticism (a graphic project). Is this an academic reality?

7   Every student understandably begins by striving after originality. After five years work he is delighted if he can attend to a simple job with scruple and insight (unless he is about to launch a successful career as a carrion artist). It helps, at least, to know that.

8   Always show discarded alternatives in support of your work. If you get stuck, develop these alternatives as far as you can.

9   If the world is crowded with inessential rubbish, is there a case for seeing what you can do with the cheapest, most simple and most ordinary materials?

10 In the first year remember that you will reject everything before you can complete it, because your values will change so fast. Can you turn this fact to positive account in the way you design? How?

11 Conceive the visible outcome of your work – including notes – as a totality; try to present a running sequential account of your thinking from beginning to end (using diagrams) for someone who doesn't know you or the problem.

12 Use colours freely in a layout pad; if you are beginning, don't sit facing tracts of empty white paper. Study the exact and detailed nature of all given factors in a job, work outwards from them.

13 If you think someone in your group has a better design concept for a job than you have, why not accept and develop it in your own way? The end-result will be very different, and a comparison valuable. You may have the best approach to the next job. Work towards objective standards.

14 In the way of samples or materials or catalogues, collect everything you like or that for some unknown reason holds your attention; not what you ought to like. Information ought to keep pace with your ability to use it.

15 If you must flip through photographs of other people's work, try this: write a short critical commentary on just one photograph, compare notes with someone. You may be surprised at what the eye and intelligence gain from *focus*.

16 Before deciding that Le Corbusier or Frank Lloyd Wright are thankfully the last of the monumental masons, hitch across Europe or America and see for yourself. On the way, get right off the beaten track and study all the most humble of human artefacts.

19 Questioning design

1   Have you considered the fine distinctions that make human faces recognizable? – the elements are as much alike, and related, as you would get from a problem analysis. So are you just beginning? How do you see a face?

2   Compare gasometers, pylons, cooling towers, street lighting. What is it about cluster high-lighting that makes the rest look sentimental?

3   If you go into a furniture shop, examine the backs and insides and know before leaving how it is (or could be) made.

4   Is a road a shallow kinetic relief? Paved with what intentions?

5   What makes a good street bollard? Geometry, surface, height, spacing, inference, articulation with the ground?

6   On what principles is a street decently furnished? What are the material ingredients?

7   Look at a car and de-gloss it in your mind's eye; what of its form is shine? What about reflection in a glass building? Compare the cut-off of high-rise buildings, vertically and horizontally. Are some visually better than others? If so, why?

8   Is a matchbox fine-tolerance cabinetmaking? Why does it work so well? When should a drawer be a tray?

9   In typography, can you see a Marxist concern for the just allocation of spaces? Or a Freudian concern with motivation and impulse? Where and how in the history of the modern movement?

10   Are milk bottles and wine bottles inferior to art glass from Finland? If so, why?

11   When a textile is used for curtains, what are its functions? What alternatives are there?

12   If you blow up a letter form and cut it out in hardboard, do you like carrying it under your arm? Try setting verse in Plantin, Univers, Bodoni; other things equal, what difference?

13   Should a table be flat? If so, why? Was Albers right to say that flush joints work in metal and not in wood? How would you make a diagram to compactly suggest the nature of wood as a material?

14   Consider noise, signal, redundance; are there distinctions here that would help you design anything?

15   What makes a Georgian sash window 'work' visually and a Victorian sash gape like a fish? How would you replace either?

16   Have you compared drinking cold water from glass, plastic, china, paper, stoneware, metal? Try listing the requirements you would need to satisfy in designing an eggcup and a teapot. Would you need to know much about the flow of liquids? What makes a bad teapot choke or drip?

17   Have you ever seen a well-designed electric fire?

18   One minute exercise: examine that old designer's friend, the Terry anglepoise lamp. Performance aside, what is glaringly inconsistent about it?

19   What is the difference between honesty and sincerity in your work?

20   If you are reorganizing your room, should you 'respect' existing dimensions? If so, why? Are there primary and secondary dimensions?

21   What is the difference between a container and an enclosure? Could it be relevant to know?

22   Would you design a prison? If not, why not?

23   Is a book a four-dimensional object? Should it be seen with x-ray eyes?

24   Can alertness be summoned and sustained by an act of will? If so, when useful?

25   Would you have preferred this book to be illustrated with comic strips? If so, why?

26   Is it good for people to stretch and reach into inconvenient places? If so, is ergonomics a science?

27   What do you like about your favourite things? Compare pubs closely. What makes a good pub? Location, publican, people who use it, decor, privacy, good beer, comfort? Also launderettes. What makes one better to be in than another? Lighting, surfaces, facilities, efficiency? How would you make one better?

28   In a café, consider the tables, etc, drawn out as a plan on your drawing board. Suppose the plan and circulation would read plausibly, the seating comfortable, yet the café is thoroughly depressing to be in. What essential decisions might be missing from your plan? (cf. Le Corbusier, 'the plan is the generator'.)

29   What is intrinsically wrong about bookcases, or questionable?

30   Is the surface the heart of things? How else will you know them?

31   Is a door handle a piece of information? What else might you prescribe for an outside door? What is a door, irreducibly?

32   Study watch and clock faces. Should a watch be round, square, or?

33   If you were visually aligning with a circle, would you wish to pick up its centre or periphery? (Other things being equal.) Could they be equal?

34   Is hard architecture male-dominated?

35   Should a well-designed ashtray conceal its contents?

36   Finally, for those who wish to ask why this book has no pictures (as some students have done), here are some reasons. Buried within them are further questions that it may be interesting to frame and ask; questions, moreover, that need answering:

a book conceived as a working tool should not be over-encumbered with precedent;

an effort of imagining, and of search, helps experience to replace consumption;

such a book enters a field to which it is merely contributory, not self-contained;

that field is already image-saturated;

this is reinforced by a tele-media culture tending always to judge by appearances;

the book argues for the primacy of meaning over appearance;

it also laments the influence of magazine and illustrative culture upon the ability of students to design from first principles;

in a book of such generality, an illustrative principle would be falsely finite, closing possibilities rather than opening them;

the book suggests that product design is less adventurous and less definitive than the design of spaces and their equipment;

however, spaces as places defy single-point perspective, needing for proper record a movie camera or supplementary drawings;

the form of a book should be at one with its message.

Strong counter-arguments can be mounted against each of these points. Do you think they manage to sustain a case?

Most of these questions have invited you to *find out* – by looking, questioning, measuring; then to *sort out* – by comparing, relating, ordering; then to *think out* against such criteria as seem relevant, in context – to make value-judgements.

This is a mouthful.

As would be a description of the designer's world. A world of seemingly disparate and unrelated things, values, interests, persons, processes. Connections have to be found, and made secure. A complex act of reconciliation has to take place; if not of the people and the stones, certainly of the people and the things.

37 Now turn to pages 110–11 (the three stages of diagnosis): a similar statement, but in a context of purpose. Does this help it to make sense?

20   Conference report

Extract from the Chairman's report on the National Conference on Art & Design Education at the Round House, London NW1, July 1968.

The Conference, which was sponsored by the Movement for Re-thinking Art and Design Education (MORADE), had two objectives:

1   to promote whatever action was seen to be called for immediately in view of the present situation in art schools throughout the country, and

2   to establish on a national scale the proper bases for further study of art & design education and of the matters that are relevant to it.

Contributors, who were drawn almost equally from the staff and students of art colleges and schools, were invited to speak freely on whatever topics they believed to be important or relevant within the general framework of the following questions:

1   Why art & design education?
2   What is a school of art? and
3   How should art schools be organized?

The Conference soon found itself to be in agreement that the purpose of art & design education is to develop critical awareness, to allow potentially creative people to develop their aptitudes, to encourage questioning and to stimulate discovery, and to promote creative behaviour. It was also generally agreed that this purpose could not be served except under conditions of freedom far greater than obtain at present – freedom from external control by bodies unsympathetic to and uncomprehending of its purpose, freedom to select students without constraint by irrelevant criteria, freedom to develop courses without regard to inappropriately academic national standards, and freedom from inhibition by too-rigid structures of internal control. The Conference recognized the urgent need for reform by the immediate removal of some impediments but it also recognized that reform in the longer term would need much further study and might well involve the reorientation of art teaching throughout the educational system as a whole. Voices were not lacking to remind the Conference of the equal need for realism.

A recurrent theme was the relationship of 'Art' to 'Society' and, therefore, of the role or roles – actual and potential – of the artist and designer today. A wide diversity of views was expressed from which it emerged that the need for solidarity in confronting a world unaware of art's value or purposes outweighed the need that might arise for distinguishing differences of function and approach between, say, 'artist' and 'designer'. It was made apparent to the Conference, by the remarks of Sir John Summerson, that even within bodies nominally constituted to represent their views there is an alarming and – in the present situation – possibly crucial lack of fundamental understanding. It was agreed by the Conference, therefore, that a primary function of art education is the extension of understanding and that a world which does not know 'what art is about' will neither be able to use it rightly nor concede to it a proper status. In this 'chicken & egg' situation the need for internal reform is paramount and urgent.

Geoffrey Bocking, Chairman

21 Matchbox maxims

or   how to keep in business as a troublemaker

:   the following could be a postscript to my book on design education & procedure

1   In this time formal education is too often a complicated game
to keep us all off the streets; soft at its centre and torpid with false
compliances.

2   Design at its best has an honourable history; affirmative, questioning, socially and personally committed, seeking to bring things
together in good sense. A very large area of this effort has degener-
ated into managerial eyewash.

3   Communication is usually a word to dignify a debasement of
language in the pursuit of profit and the avoidance of plain speaking in social transactions. Academically, communication theory is
interesting where it is intelligible. A poet might recoil from communication theory as from a natural enemy.

4   Formal education, design, communication, must now argue for
their life and there is nothing self-evident in the claims of these
activities as now studied or practised.

5   Search: for credibility and a principle (not less a fact) of necessity in the roots of our work. It is not difficult to be personally creative whilst culturally inconsequent.

6   Any possible structure for education must be seen, and experienced, as an accessible hypothesis; argued out and acted out in that
way; tested close to destruction – certainly to continuous renewal.

7   Art and design (as fields of application) are as near together, and as different, as priest and doctor would be if we could still respect a priestly function. A philosophy – a philosopher – is a man of words.

When we feel threatened, in ourselves or in society, the concerns of each may seem identical; and the conditions for health – survival – may seem to lie elsewhere.

8   Ask if your environment is strictly necessary – excepting food, warmth, shelter, friends. As rhetoric, this is a satisfactory way to start. It is also one basis for work assessment.

9   Lethaby: 'design, indeed, design that is really fresh and penetrating, coexists, it seems, only with the simplest conditions'. Consistently, he might now add 'recovered and tempered virtue in well-doing'. What are our conditions for coexistence?

11   For those who want to investigate in their work, as well as to experiment, an intermediate technology is not to be despised.

12   An open hand is a better image than a closed fist.

From each of these remarks I hope you may find at least one good question.

This statement was issued in 1972 to precede a series of lectures to art schools.

10   Omitted here for reasons of possible defamation.

22 The Bristol experiment

The brief notes that follow concern two phases of the Construction School (1964–79), originally of the West of England College of Art. The work of the School was fully documented, but a detailed account would be out of place here.

The School was established by a team of eight people from London (mostly from the Royal College of Art) including a philosopher and an English language specialist, supported, informally, by a group of architects and designers sympathetic to its aims. The work of the group was grafted on to an existing small school of furniture design, with excellent craft traditions, the Head of which (Dennis Darch) now became Convenor of the new school of design. Richard Hollis came as a member of the team to head the then Graphic School, which combined with Construction in a common first year. The group had no career interest in teaching at that time (some members later developed such an interest), but was strongly motivated to explore the following aims: to found a design institute with a teaching component for DipAD, the teaching staff continuing in design practice; to set up a three-year design course without specialization, leading to various areas of design including possibly architecture; and as a school, to set about re-examining certain assumptions or postulates of the modern movement in design. This was a necessary task for design education in 1964 (if not perennially so), following the work of the Hochschule für Gestaltung Ulm. For certain good reasons (including the skills, equipment, and traditions available) the School concentrated on one-off jobs and special equipment ('problems in which place and occasion were active determinants'[!]) – thus linking to architecture – with the graphic work providing a product-design component in its thinking. Political realities led to the almost immediate abandonment of the institute as an aim; for similar reasons, the intended hospitality to European and American designers had to be curtailed, though interesting work was done with designers such as Paul Schuitema from the Netherlands.

The group became interested in a course which, in content, sequence, and outcome, could be irreducibly relevant to designers in all subsequent fields of specialization; both with respect to knowledge and technique. Thus a five-year course was postulated, the School providing the first three, with an optional postgraduate specialization or the alternative of design office practice: the three years providing an employable competence. Following the principle usefully and pithily described by Bruce Archer, that designers should be 'jacks of all trades but master of one', technical studies were built around timber practice and technology, for which the teaching skills were available. However, all projects or specialized areas of study were intentionally referred back as 'limited cases of general principles', so that at this time there was no craft bias in the work of the School; indeed rather the reverse. Accepting students from a foundation course that was usually fine-art based, the Construction first year (combined with graphics) was allowed to be intellectually demanding in contrast, being largely concerned with problem-solving, and with communication technique. The second year opened out into workshop practice and technical studies in wood, metals, and plastics. The third year joined with graphics students again in exhibition design, but was intentionally student-designed around a series of options that brought together and developed the work of the first and second year. In practice, however, the year had to become 'furniture design' because the School had meanwhile been recognized for this subject. Despite a most detailed academic programme (which no one could be found to contest), a highly organized school, enthusiastic staff and students, and new buildings and equipment, recognition was at that time confined to specific categories (the relevance of which it was the purpose of the School to challenge) and in an Alice-like academic world the School had to apply for recognition in interior design, which it did not intend to teach, this being the only category with a five-year expectation. In the event, furniture design was awarded, thus depriving the School of the student intake that would make the best sense of its aims, and necessarily altering its subsequent direction. A national petition, strongly supported by architects particularly, failed to shift this position. The School therefore set up a parallel senior vocational course, starting in the workshops and crossing with the DipAD students half-way. Given excellent students and a stream of supporting visitors, the School was able to make the most of its situation, morale was high, and much interesting work was undertaken. Development at the level, and of the kind, at first intended, was not of course possible. In 1968/9 (when I left) the School was able to offer hospitality to Hornsey and Guildford students, and to contribute support to the international student movement of that time.

For the second phase for which I returned to the School (from 1975 to 1977) – being on this occasion 'voted in' by staff and students – the historical situation, and terms of reference, were very different, and harder to describe in a short space. Various things had gone wrong, morale was low, and the School had lost energy and direction. It was decided to put people and relationships first, in a reorganization that diversified the potential of the School into autonomous groups or communes (intentional communities). Each was to specialize according to the experience and competence of the full-time member of staff in charge; each combined first, second, and third year, in such a way that learning by a form of osmosis could occur in each group; and each built and equipped its own studio environment (sharing technical facilities). The groups were intentionally co-operative within their own family structure, but to some extent competitive within the central area (the arena) where work from all groups was exhibited and criticized, and from which individual student progress was monitored from the standpoint of CNAA requirements. The arena was to be one of critical disputation, but it also had certain co-ordinating and specialized functions (as for tutorials). The Head of the School worked from the arena, with others, but the arena had no power to overrule a genuine autonomy in the groups, which could devise their own working methods (but expect them to be defensible).

Among the objects of this non-heirarchic organization were: the fostering of a student-based and a much more variegated working basis for the School, the mustering and focusing of all available energies in ways that would be at once a challenge and informally derived, the improvement of working and personal relationships all round, the productive working-out of certain internalized tensions that had developed in the School, and a move to make the Head of School rather less indispensable than formerly, his position

166

becoming a critical function and a co-ordinating one. In many ways this experiment proved interesting. Unfortunately a severe staff cut removed the part-time staff who should have circulated between the groups, helping to cross-fertilize ideas, and whose energies were really essential to the success of autonomous grouping; and the School found itself in a vulnerable position for a return visit from the CNAA (having obtained initial support for the experiment in 1976), who did not feel in 1979 that the group system had sufficiently vindicated its rather doubtful promise. At this stage the School was ended (except for those students completing studies).

In retrospect, what did the School achieve? As designers such as Robin Day and Terence Conran were quick to acknowledge, the standard of work was very high in the first phase (though probably too much staff-influenced), and the social structure of the School and its increasingly student-centred learning were the notable contributions of its second phase. In both, the standard of consciousness, of critical discussion, were remarked as being exceptional; and relationships were normally accepted as being adult and responsible even in times of gloom. It could be said, I think with fairness, that when the School was failing it was beyond an average mark-up for success; and this, if true, is greatly to its credit. The employment record for students has been very good and very diverse; an artisan interest has led to several workshops, but without (numerically) a bias in that direction. The School always put architecture first in its design studies, as distinct from its own typical products, and had unusual support from designers in that field; including in the early days Jim Stirling, Peter Burberry, and Richard Rogers, and continuing later with visitors as diverse as Walter Segal, Colin Ward, Ted Cullinan, and John Miller. Colin Boyne (of the *Architects' Journal*) once noted that the first-phase course seemed a very likely foundation for architecture. It is a pity that this bridge-building could not have been taken further (partly for the reasons already given). It has been observed that even emancipated architects tend to distance themselves from 'design' and lean rather heavily on the status-reassurance of their profession; if the work of the School did something to reveal and diminish this problem, this has been a helpful contribution.

Finally, it might be said that an obstinate habit of mind emerged, following Rilke's precept 'hold to the difficult'; in playing it the hard way, the School was always vulnerable, both internally and to the outside world. However, like the AA School of Architecture (with which the Construction School probably had more in common than with most design schools elsewhere), it would be hard for a student to leave without in some useful sense knowing the score. To this extent, at its best, the School suffered the real world. Three prospectus sayings: 'our position is ranged-left and open-ended'; 'putting things together in ways that make sense'; and 'design is a field of concern, response, and enquiry, as often as decision and consequence'.

23   Text references

These references give the source for (where it exists in printed form), or otherwise qualify, material quoted in the text of the book. Place of publication is London, unless otherwise indicated.

6   *Le Corbusier*: from 'If I had to teach you architecture', *Focus* (no. 1, summer 1938, p. 12). The article is now reprinted in: Dennis Sharp (ed.), *The rationalists* (Architectural Press, 1978).

6   *Conrad*: *Victory*; it is Heyst speaking.

6   *Woolley*: in *Anarchy* (no. 97).

8   *Schumacher*: from *Good work* (Sphere Books, 1980, pp. 29–30).

21   *Vitruvius/Wotton*: Sir Henry Wotton, *The elements of architecture* (1624).

21   *Reich*: epitaph to *The function of the orgasm* (Panther Books, 1968).

31   'freedom': a frequent reference in this text, but not for me to circumscribe. For the distinction from 'liberty', consult Herbert Read's discussion of the matter in *Anarchy and order* (Faber & Faber, 1945), M. L. Berneri's useful *Journey through Utopia* (Routledge & Kegan Paul, 1950), and Erich Fromm's *Fear of freedom* and *The sane society* (Routledge & Kegan Paul, 1942 and 1956).

36   *Gropius*: see, for example, *The new architecture and the Bauhaus* (Faber & Faber, 1935, p. 92).

37   *Auden*: the lines on 'new styles of architecture' are from 'Petition', first published in his *Poems* (1930) – and not reprinted in all later collections.

38   *Frankl*: see *Man's search for meaning* (Hodder & Stoughton, 1963).

39   *Large*: *Sugar in the air* (Jonathan Cape, 1937), seriously due for a reprint – there is nothing of the kind quite so well made.

40   *Berger*: for example, *Ways of seeing* (BBC / Penguin, 1972).

43   *Schuitema*: from 'A statement', *Circuit* (magazine of the West of England College of Art, autumn 1966, pp. 1, 5). See also his

article 'New typographical design in 1930', *New Graphic Design* (no. 11, December 1961, pp. 16–19).

63 *Medawar*: see *Induction and intuition in scientific thought* (Methuen, 1969).

63 *Popper*: critics and others who lean upon (their interpretation of) the words of this philosopher, will note the absence of a text reference. In my opinion, Popper is a philosopher's philosopher. I lack the training to estimate the correctness (or otherwise) of his views. Some philosophers (including, oddly enough, Wittgenstein) have the mysterious gift of lay accessibility.

73 *Lethaby*: in A. R. N. Roberts, *William Richard Lethaby 1857–1931* (LCC Central School of Arts & Crafts, 1957, p. 48).

77 *Newman*: quoted by J. W. N. Sullivan, *Beethoven* (Jonathan Cape, 1927, p. 9).

78 *Whitehead*: from *The aims of education* (Williams & Norgate, 1929, p. 18).

90 *Turner*: from *Orpheus or the music of the future* (Routledge & Kegan Paul [1926] p. 19).

91 *Ashbee on Geddes*: from *A Palestine notebook 1918–23*, and quoted by Paddy Kitchen in *A most unsettling person* (Gollancz, 1975, pp. 299, 300).

91 *Geddes on Mackintosh*: quoted by Paddy Kitchen in *A most unsettling person* (p. 149).

91 *Ashbee*: the earlier statement is from *An endeavour towards the teaching of John Ruskin & William Morris* (Edward Arnold, 1901); both this and the passage from *Should we stop teaching art?* are quoted by Pevsner in *Pioneers of modern design* (Harmondsworth: Penguin Books, 1960, p. 26).

92 *Mumford*: cf. his introduction to the 1957 edition of Lethaby's *Form in civilization* (Oxford University Press, 1957, p. xiii).

92 *Lethaby*: aphorisms, in Roberts (as above, pp. 64, 65, 72).

92 *Gropius*: see his contribution to *Herbert Read: a memorial symposium* edited by Robin Skelton (Methuen, 1970).

93 *Read*, 'A song for the Spanish anarchists', from his *Collected poems* (Faber & Faber, 1966, pp. 149–50), and quoted with permission of David Higham Associates.

125 'survey before plan': the title of a series of books published by Lund Humphries for the Association for Planning and Regional

Reconstruction; see, for example, *The hub of the house* (no. 2, 1945) edited by E. M. Willis.

125   'the plan is the generator': Le Corbusier, *Towards a new architecture* (John Rodker, 1927).

134   *Richards*: from *Practical criticism* (Routledge & Kegan Paul, 1929, p. 182).

168   *Rilke*: from *Letters to a young poet* (Sidgwick & Jackson, 1945).

Afterword

Norman Potter wrote the first version of this book in the 1960s. When, in 1968, the political landscape of the world suffered tremors – the May 'events' in Paris, the Prague 'spring' of revolt against a Stalinist regime, the great demonstrations in cities across the world against the American war in Vietnam – his work changed course. In England the events of that year included the occupation of the art schools at Hornsey (north London) and Guildford (in Surrey, to the south of London). These happenings were at once calls for abolition of decrepit authority in the microcosm of those schools, and part of the larger, world-wide movement for renewal. As he mentions in his account of the Construction School at Bristol (part 22), Potter gave up teaching then. He joined the student occupation at Hornsey and took part in its constructive educational-political agitations. He finished *What is a designer* in the intense atmosphere of those months of 1968. The following year, 1969, the book was published by the firm of Studio Vista in London, within their small-format series of works on art and design, edited by John Lewis.

What is a designer is certainly a book of '1968'. But it is more than this, and its more general, longer-lasting reference is why the book is still current. Ten years on from its first publication, I worked as editor and publisher with Potter on a second edition. We doubled its extent, adding much factual reference material, as well as revising and updating its arguments. This edition was published by Hyphen Press (from an address in Reading, England) in 1980, just at the onset of postmodernism in architecture, design, and culture more generally. This second edition thus took on something of the colour of that moment of '1980': when a Conservative government, under the leadership of Margaret Thatcher, had just come to power in Britain. Or, rather, Potter wrote in defence and explanation of a continuing modern movement, in the face of the turns and shifts of that time.

In its very specific information – most obviously in the lists of organizations, with addresses and telephone numbers – this second

173

edition of the book was an attempt to represent the specificity of design. It is part of the nature of the practice of design that it swings, sometimes from minute to minute, from the very specific (a phone number, indeed, or a screw size) to the very general (for example, good form in a curving surface or the ethics of designing for an oil company). And in his book, from sentence to sentence, Norman Potter would often travel between these two dimensions. But in books, as in life, particularity goes out of date, sometimes very rapidly.

At the end of the 1980s, in what now seemed to be a ten-year cycle of revision, we made a third edition of *What is a designer*. This incorporated another revision of specific information. Norman Potter also wrote a new introduction, reflecting on the period of the 1980s, and affirming his wish not to change what he had written. We published this edition as a prelude to making another book, *Models & Constructs*, in which Potter presented his own work as a maker – a 'cabinetmaker', to oversimplify – and as a poet. Readers interested in his life and work – about which the self-effacing *What is a designer* does not give much clue – are referred to this other book, published in 1990. Norman Potter died in 1995, leaving *Models & Constructs* as his main public statement, though with enough material in typescript to make at least another book of writings about designing and making.

Towards the end of the 1990s, when *What is a designer* was again out of print, plans began to be made for Spanish and Danish editions of the book. This drew attention to another aspect of the book's particularity of discussion – its references to British conditions. Potter was a strong internationalist, but also clear about rooting his discussion in the particular context in which he found himself. Ideally one would make a book that provided specific references (organizations, books, other resources) for each language community. But the realistic course was followed: to cut the purely local, British material, with no attempt at substitution. And this 'international' text is the one given here in the present edition.

The simplest course has been followed. Thus, one chapter, or 'part' as we call them in this book (the word is less literary, more something of the workshop) has been excised. This is the discussion titled 'Design education: practice (GB)', which followed the part on 'Design education: principles': bringing the grand ideas down to earth, with a truth-telling bump. Those who want to read Potter's splendidly acerbic remarks on 'course validation' and other troubles of British education must now seek out a copy of the second or third edition of this book. The predominantly British list of useful addresses has been lost too. Other local discussion, here and there, has been cut. But at least some of the more specific, national and time-bound material has been retained for its intrinsic interest: the discussion of reading (part 7), the conference report (part 19), the account of the Construction School at Bristol (part 22). The introduction that Norman Potter wrote for the 1989 edition is also given here, with the loss of two paragraphs specifically about the 1980s.

One further kind of modification has seemed necessary, to keep up with technical change in the world. Thus, since the last revision of 1989, the typewriter has been all but replaced by word-processing on the personal computer. Norman Potter was devoted to the typewriter, as an instrument for ordering thought, and for production of texts. With regret, his discussion of the machine, in 'Simple graphics: a strategy' (part 12), has been altered. The discussion of libraries has been cut altogether: the nature of libraries has changed too much. This prompts the thought that the best provision of current information, such as Potter wanted in this book, is now to be found through the internet.

So *What is a designer* appears again in this new form, six years after its author's death. I suppose that Norman Potter would have been amused by this continuation of his engagement with design, which was always questioning, never merely professional or a matter of simple assumption. It must have been in the early 1990s, irritated by some unspeakable new manifestation of 'the design business', when he remarked to me that, if we ever made a new edition of the book, the title would have to become 'What *was* a designer'. But the title stays as it is: a question, a proposition, a hand reached out – to engage 'students of all ages'.

Robin Kinross
London, June 2001

Index of names

This index lists names of people and corporate institutions mentioned in the text; those referred to as authors of a book (and in no other context) are not included.